THROUGH THE VEILS OF MYSTERY

INTO THE DEPTHS
AN EXPLORATION OF INVISIBLE
INNER REALMS

KRISTINA BAZAN

THOUGHT
CATALOG
Books

THOUGHTCATALOG.COM

Published by Thought Catalog Books, an imprint of Thought Catalog, a digital magazine owned and operated by The Thought & Expression Co. Inc., an independent media organization founded in 2010 and based in the United States of America. For stocking inquiries, contact stockists@shopcatalog.com.

Produced by Chris Lavergne and Noelle Beams
Layout by Thought Catalog Books
Circulation management by Isidoros Karamitopoulos

thoughtcatalog.com | shopcatalog.com

International edition, printed internationally and fulfilled by Amazon in select countries. The limited, original print edition remains available to order and ships worldwide from ShopCatalog.com.

ISBN 978-1-949759-69-3

To Love.

INTRODUCTION

☽ ☼ ☾

Back in late 2019, I experienced what some would call a "spiritual awakening." I had personally never really heard about that term before, nor had I been working towards experiencing something of this nature. It just so happened that I came to a point in my human adventure where many things I had been building for years came crashing down: business contracts, friendships, romantic love. It was a proper "Tower" moment as depicted by the Tarot de Marseille, a crashing and crumbling of old structures that were no longer serving my well-being. And even that last part took me a while to understand as I thought I was doing great when in fact, I was running on empty for years and periodically burning myself out. That tower moment has gotten me completely broken. Later I found out: I was cracked open. But we'll get to that part.

During that time, I found myself meditating properly for the first time in my life as I slept on the floor of my living room for 10 days, unable to do anything. Meditation was the only thing that soothed the psychological pressure and overall heartache I felt. My way of meditating at that time was very pragmatic. I would meditate exactly like I would do everything else back in early 2019: with a goal in mind and the priority of efficiency at all costs. Later on, I discovered Vipassana meditation which became a tremendous guiding tool to navigate through my inner space. From the edge of my awareness, I could sense that beyond the protective walls I had built all around myself to keep me safe was a vastness, an infinity beyond anything I could name with accurate words. And I could sense that this infinity was what some mystics call Samadhi or the absolute essence of all, which is: Love with a capital L. Unconditional love. Beyond any and all conditions. Social, economic, political, logical, rational conditions. Like the water pouring out of a fresh source, satisfying the thirst of a wanderer lost in the desert. There I was thirsty for God, Goddess, for my own infinite nature. There I was, laying on my floor, unable to cope with reality, and for the first time in my life, I truly began to silently say to myself from within:

I have nothing to lose. Nothing.

I said this repeatedly about 50 times or more. Feeling it throughout my body. Feeling the resonance and the intention of these words surging through me like honey nectar. It was moving through me like a current. The more I said it, the more I heard it echo within me, the more my body would let go and I could allow myself to relax into this powerful declaration. I have nothing to lose. Tears were rolling down my cheeks. Sadness was mixing and merging now with a new sense of freedom. Eventually, joy came through as one of the deepest feelings of surrender I've permitted myself to really feel into in a very, very long time. As this happened, what felt like a massive current of absolute electricity surged through and just blasted the space between my eyebrows wide open. At that time, I didn't properly know that this space was called the third eye. I began to see colors, visions, and a kaleidoscopic spectacle while being fully awake. I was in a state of awe, and yet my body was so relaxed that I couldn't move, just observing the bright colors that started creating shapes around me. I had my eyes closed yet was fully aware that I wasn't asleep. I was submerged in this dance of the divine in pure ecstatic bliss as my grief and sorrow exploded in a million dancing particles of mirroring colors revealing themselves to me beyond the curtain of my eyelids and the veils of this reality.

The current began moving from the space between my eyebrows to the very bottom of my body, unlocking with a high-frequency voltage each section of my body as if it was asleep this whole time. I saw wheels of energy throughout the length of my spine swirling and opening. I saw images of a fountain whose pipes were getting unblocked, unclogged and the water just started bursting like a storm. Out of nowhere, I began to move as if I was going through an actual exorcism. At this point, I'll admit I started to freak out a little bit. Simply because I had never moved in such a way before. Ever. I felt like an animal. Like a panther in the jungle. Stretching my vertebrae one by one in the deepest, most delectable way possible. It was so deeply delicious, and yet in this deep bliss was also such a deep intensity that I felt like I was going to blast out of my body.

At this point, I started opening my eyes and breathing loudly. All my instincts had awoken, and I began singing. Singing sounds that made no sense to my logical mind, and yet my whole being understood each sound coming through, like light codes and ancient incantations that were sending shivers through all my tissues. An aspect of my consciousness was so scared of dying; it really felt like I was dying, and truly: that's what was happening. It was a complete rebirth, a deep purification and shedding of that which was perpetu-ating the illusion of any separation from the divine, love and God. After the singing had stopped, I was immersed in absolute silence and a total void. It felt so warm and nurtur-ing and yet empty and endless. I saw two numbers emerging from the void: 0 & 1, and clearly heard zero is the womb of all, the receptor, and 1 is the light of all, the vector. Together and within their union, all Creation is.

I then saw rays of bright blue light. It's almost like these rays were encircling me in the energy of an immense grace. These rays telepathically spoke to me through my aware-ness and came to nurture me like a child being born. These rays of blue light felt so alive, like actual beings, elongated and sleek. I felt their energy which was so profoundly sa-cred and benevolent. Intuitively I knew, without a single doubt, that I could surrender and trust, so I just allowed myself to let go of trying to analyze or categorize the situ-ation. I was in deep reverence and felt so much energy moving through me. I could really feel how they saw ALL of me. Even the spaces within my consciousness where I was trying to hide. These rays guided me and explained to me what I was experiencing. And then they showed me. They showed me everything. They showed me how light creates this reality: weaving each filament into one another like a tapestry, a fluid so thin it feels like matter, but it is actually photons of light reverberating upon one another. I saw how our bodies are maps and how emotions (energy + motion) are crystalized and create patterns that can be energetically seen from higher dimensions. I was shown how absolutely everything is alive, all elements, the trees, from the biggest to the tiniest rocks: all is living conscious-ness densified at certain speeds of frequency and light. I saw how our nervous system interacts with other particles of light generating energetic reactions, or as the rays of light described it: music and symphonies.

They said something I loved: we aren't victims; we are creators. Humans love to call themselves imperfect, the word being used to mainly justify a deep denial of its own creative power misuse and abuse, mainly from the level of thoughts, beliefs, and projections. I was shown how many people think that what they think or believe is "private," and so they hold grudges, nurture jealousy within themselves, and give way too much space to their inner critic to destroy their self-confidence. In fact, none of our beliefs are private, for they are all connected to a collective unified field that generates an etheric layer around Earth called the Astral plane. Our beliefs are connected to somewhat of a collective voting system. The Universe is neutral in its way of reflecting the meaning we assimilate unto it. For example, if you genuinely believe the Universe is generous, you will experience life's generosity. However the more people feel desperate, depressed, and energetically think thoughts such as: this life sucks, why is it so hard, this world is unfair, the more this is what actually manifests as the Universe processes these energetic votes and therefore reflects back these initial statements. Imagine being a painter and standing in front of a white canvas: each statement you make will create a ripple of color, a shape. If you are thinking "*I hate my life*" this is the energy you will project on the canvas, and this is the piece of art you will get in the end, a painting depicting your hate which is what currently happens a lot as we see pain becoming glamorized in modern culture. In psychological terms, this is called a bias. You are the one assigning meaning, you are the one continuously choosing your perspective and, therefore, also experiencing it.

The internal or so-called "private" beliefs of each individual influence our collective reality. Where energy (focus/concentration) grows, energy flows. If many people believe life is hard, that belief will manifest on a societal level as many have been energetically voting for that reality. The manifestation is the result of the belief, although many think the opposite. Indeed most people think that their beliefs are simply shaped by daily life occurrences. This typically is a victim mentality, for it is saying that you are a victim of circumstances and have no say in how things energetically operate within and all around you. If your belief system is based on a default reality: then you must look into what this default is and if it is serving your well-being. Don't just accept the way things are. You have an energetic vote in all this. In truth, there is no beginning and no end: everything is energy.

I then heard clearly: humanity is perfect, it simply keeps abusing itself on and on again, and that is why it abuses others. It is still at the kindergarten level of its own energy management, for it still believes that to have more it needs to take from somewhere outside of itself. This couldn't be further away from the truth. All beings, all particles have a still point, and from that still point, all energy and re-sources can be accessed. Very much like the eye of a storm, a place where absolute calm abides even amidst a tornado. Humanity is learning harmonious energetic mastery, which involves realizing that this is a fractal reality where every-thing is interconnected. The Universe takes everything into account: our emotional undulations, our belief patterns, our thoughts, that which we feed within, that which we starve. We have entire worlds living inside of us, just like we live in a vast Universe. Both are reflections of one another. Just think about everything that is beyond our vision and beyond the known spectrum.

Humans truly are like the most beautiful and unique musical instruments. You are energetic beings that have manifested in a realm of physicality to experience this aspect of your wholeness. And by virtue of being in this realm, you have the responsibility of maintaining energetic hygiene. You must realize you are absolutely perfect, especially because you have the option to experience what seems like "mistakes" from your localized vantage point of awareness. Mistakes are simply "missed takes" in creating harmony and coherence. For example, when you play music, you might hit some disharmonious chords from time to time while exploring different chord progressions.

Our nervous system is like a constellation of infinite possibilities and probabilities, and each time we make a decision, new neural pathways light up in our brains, and these pathways mimic those we see in the sky: just like coordinates on the map of the infinite ocean of consciousness. The infinity that consciousness is is ever-expanding, and everything you choose to experience is simultaneously experienced by the whole universe itself, for we are an interconnected ecosystem continuously self-discovering itself. Many people have been stubbornly looping on the same neural pathways, not wanting to change their ways of operating. It is like forcing a brick wall to crack.

The number one thing we must collectively understand is that the Universe is very much like a biofeedback hologram. Whatever we vibrate (our vibration being the composition of many elements) is ultimately what our reality will reflect, and there are many layers to that. We must have tremendous compassion and appreciation for our human experience, which is so detailed, so subtle, and so complex. Being here trains us to truly become energetic ninjas, and it isn't for the faint of heart, as life on Earth involves many profoundly intense and difficult experiences. It is part of the deal when incarnating here; Earth is like an energetic university.

All the answers were within all along. We weren't born with a guidebook because we have the guidebook within. And we find it when we realize that we are life itself; we are the captains of our ships as we sail through the ocean of consciousness. Life forges our discernment. Indeed all the keys, all the tools, have been in us all along, right in the dormant aspects of our consciousness, of our brains and DNA. That is where the spiritual gold is accessed and where the greatest mysteries of our collective humanity are retrieved. Right within our hidden inner realms. Hidden because we chose to experience human incarnation as a quantum quest and chose to hide the truth about our origins away from ourselves. Because we voluntarily, out of gentleness for our human nervous system, chose to forget our past lives each time we reincarnate to continue adventuring with a clean slate. Because we voluntarily chose to deny reincarnation to focus on this very life as the most precious thing in the world without thinking we'll get another chance at it in another life. In fact, there is today so much documented proof of reincarnation. You can read the books "Children Who Remember Previous Lives" by Ian Stevenson M.D, "Journey of the Soul" by Michael Newton PhD, or look up the fascinating story of James Leininger. Because we voluntarily chose to believe dogmatic spiritual doctrines that disconnected us from our own direct connection with our hearts, our wisdom, our discernment and God to forge radical discernment in our journeying through contrasts. It is possible to retrieve these memories, and many people do. We, humans, are made of hues: expressive colors beaming through our auras with each thought, each feeling, each response. The truth is we are light beings, made of filaments of light. We are light itself. Unlimited creation itself. With each choice we make, infinite branches of probabilities open up.

The blue rays showed me how everything is an expression of light, including what we call darkness. Darkness is light particles vibrating very slowly and isn't to be confused with evil. Evil and darkness are two completely different things; they highlighted this many times as this is still a very prevalent confusion amongst us all. There is a big difference between the principles of darkness, represented mostly by the feminine womb of creation, also corresponding to the void field, nothingness and silence, all of which are regenerative components of our Universe. Yet evil, which again we often confuse with darkness, is an act of harm towards self or others usually accompanied by the enjoyment or pleasure of doing so.

Indeed, even the void consists of energy. It is a very slow and absorbent energy field. These blue beams of light invited me to write down what they had to share with me, and I filled up 4 entire notebooks with things I had never heard of before. To this day, there are things in these notebooks I still don't fully understand with my mind but I know them to be profoundly true with all of my heart. The words I wrote in these notebooks are the basis for *this* text. In these notebooks I wrote down formulas, equations, and information regarding the way our multiverse operates. I was shown visually (telepathically as well as through my third eye) what the fractal nature of reality is, and how the whole is contained in everything. I was shown how our body is a template. I was told about kinetic energy and especially about the energetic meridians of our bodies and how we have the power to truly manifest miracles. I was shown how our hands are a fractal of our feet, of our ears, of our gut and that our whole system is mirroring itself. That is why in certain holistic medicinal practices, such as in the Chinese ear seeding healing technique, you put little seeds on very specific points of the ear to treat the whole body: because it is a fractal and everything is interconnected. We still haven't tapped entirely into the dormant aspects of our consciousness and our brain's full capacities. They communicated to me that this is changing and that humanity is awakening. Awakening is primarily activating the dormant areas of the brain and creating co-herence with the heart space: which creates a resonance and a very powerful magnetic field. We are both magnetic (feminine principle-attraction-inner) and electric (mascu-line-projection-outer) beings. Coherence between the heart and mind is basically an alignment of wishes, beliefs, and values. Many people vibrate in complete dissonance: their heart wants one thing while their brain wants something completely different, and so their manifested reality reflects an absolute mess, deep confusion, and the experience of being "lost." We are never lost: we are simply continuously buffering our inner coherence and refining our intentions. And not to mention the crucial importance of the gut in all this, which is very much like a third brain.

MRI brain scans have already shown what happens when Buddhist monks are meditating: their brains light up. These scans have also been done on famous psychics, people able to look internally through their inner channels into different vibrational timelines (just like an energetic forecast) and make some predictions as they tap into the vibrational field of expanding probabilities. Very specific areas of the brain light up when they are receiving and channeling the information. Very much like a radio station, the mind attunes itself to certain frequencies and becomes a channel. We are in the process of integration and becoming conscious of who we really are and our great dormant capabilities. We are in the process of remembering our Oneness after a long time of collective spiritual self-denial and dogmatic thinking, which made us believe that our life here was a punishment and a separation from our true original home.

*We are here to master conscious
manifestation and to do it within a state
of peace and profound respect for all.*

I then took a large piece of paper and was shown my life in the format of a map. The blue beings guided me to write certain numbers and certain geometric shapes, and I just understood everything it meant. I also want to specify how I was shown the absolute importance of Christ consciousness as the central sun of our soul and how it goes way beyond any dogmatic belief system. The Christ energy is the balance of polarities, and that very still point in the middle of opposing forces: the eye of the storm where peace continuously abides. You can imagine it as the very central part at the middle of a compass, it is both the manifested and un-manifested, the direction and the stillness. It is unconditional love itself.

I understood how my life was like a galaxy, how with each decision, we travel through space/time and how space/time is simply consciousness experiencing itself through the vastness of an infinite field of creative possibilities and energetic combinations mirrored as pathways in our nervous system. In truth, neither space nor time truly exist because Source, Energy, the Universe, God, Goddess is the single, zero still point, the beyond, the Everything and the Nothing from which all realities emerge: all rays of light. That's the eternal paradox, the absolute mystery.

I was asking questions, trying to understand why so many of us struggle, and I was shown very, very clearly how everything, and I do mean *everything*, is absolute unconditional love. It can be hard to understand, but even the worst things that happen in this world are done in the name of love (or the denial of it) because true love allows for experience to occur. Experience sharpens discernment, and discernment allows for smoother navigation in the field. It might seem sadistic at first but from the ultimate perspective of the Universe, it is simply allowing. We are the actors of our play. Unconditional Love in its higher states can be neutral as to what its expression chooses and allows in terms of experiences. They gave me this analogy: imagine parents bringing their hyperactive, hungry-for-life 3-year-old toddler to play with other kids in a park. Imagine if every single time the child tried to run around to do something new, to experience, and to make mistakes, the parents would stand behind them, forbidding every single risky move. We get mad at the Universe or God for allowing us to even have the option of making mistakes, but we are like kids learning how to manage our energy, and that is a gift in and of itself; otherwise, we would have simply remained in etheric form. We manifested this physical reality as an absolute miraculous expression of the divine in form, and a truly beautiful space for experiences to occur. And for physicality to occur: contrast must exist. And with contrast comes love and hate, good and bad, yes and no.

They also showed me and highlighted how twisted and deviated our understanding of love currently is because we have been in such deep self-sabotaging patterns that our ability to respond, our sense of responsibility has been corrupted; we forgot that we are entirely the creators of our reality, absolutely one hundred percent sovereign. We are on a living, breathing playground, and instead of respecting and honoring the field, we have been fighting with each other continuously, stealing, raping, abusing, and hurting ourselves and others. Most importantly, we have been betraying ourselves and our boundaries.

The truth is we have been fighting within ourselves. Yet imagine, truly think about it for a second: what would life be like if mistakes, or what we consider mistakes, weren't allowed in this vibrational reality? What would art be? What would relationships be? What would music be? What would experimentation be? You might think: *Well, I'd be perfectly fine! I'd live a trauma-free life, that's what it would be like.* Think again. A life where missed takes simply don't exist would be very bland. Sports wouldn't exist (imagine golfing without the option of missing a take), music wouldn't exist, chess, literature, and art. Everything in our world is a reflection of our inner self explorations; everything we see from the chair to the door, to your window was originally an idea in someone's mind. Perhaps the issue is that we judge ourselves so harshly when mistakes are simply re-directions throughout the infinite pathways within our inner invisible realms. This doesn't mean we shouldn't strive to optimize our energetic usage and specifically make abuse completely obsolete: by making it so clear for everyone that everything they are looking for and the path to their inner well-being is of their choosing and it happens in them, through them. People can guide you, like teachers, doctors, and health professionals do. But no one can walk for you. No one can feel what you feel. You hold the reins. And it first begins with a choice.

When I was a child, I had a near-death accident and had a glimpse at the beyond. I peeked beyond the veils and saw what appeared like the incarnation tunnel. It looked like a vortex of light. It's a vision that always stayed with me. I was shown how people are even more scared of life, of truly deeply living, loving, opening up, scared of their own true power, of their sexuality and deep unconditional love itself, much more than death which most people consider to be an exit door. Of course, many of us fear these last few moments before death actually occurs, yet as Deepak Chopra so wisely says in one of his talks: *Death is simply the continuation of life. There is no escaping yourself.* His whole book "Life After Death" talks specifically about this.

I was shown how our deepest, truest wishes are our destiny and our hardships are the guardians testing our will to see how strong our faith, and our belief in ourselves is. Faith is the essential key in any process. It is faith that gives the runner the power to finish a marathon, it is faith that guides the scientist to keep researching to find optimized solutions even when they seem impossible, it is faith that inspires the artist to keep creating after endless rejections, it is faith that keeps us going. Now mark these words, for they are very important; you make your fate, your choices draw your path. You are the choice, you are the path. Faith will lead you forward. This is a deep process of refinement. Perhaps our collective traumas are the greatest catalysts of our adventures, for diamonds are born from pressure. This doesn't mean we should seek to generate trauma for the means of learning. Instead, we can accept that it was a necessary path to forge ourselves into individuals aware of the energetic ripples of every single one of our inner movings. We can, with inner maturity, learn through grace and in love, honoring what is, without the need to manifest trauma for us to understand something. You see, in my experience, life had to destroy so much in my life for me to finally accept my spiritual gifts which I had rejected for so long. I was so focused on social approval, status, pleasing people, and material success without the foundation of physical/mental/ spiritual health to support it. I couldn't, by all means, let these things go, as my professional ambition made me hold on to these things for dear life with all my might. So life had to force me into it, and it wasn't gentle. It was literally a rescue mission that only manifested because the deepest parts of myself called upon it as I always knew, from the bottom of my heart, there was so much more to life. It doesn't make you tough, endurant, or truly successful to reach your professional goals at the detriment of your spiritual, mental, and physical health. It doesn't serve you to hurt yourself on your way towards achieving your dreams.

Our intentions orient the course of our quest in certain specific directions, and so we adventure through the vastness of creative choices we get to make daily, hour by hour, second by second. And you reading this is surely no coincidence. Nothing is a coincidence; everything is a sign on your roadmap.

Indeed, there is a diamond with infinite facets within ourselves, and these facets often negotiate together. We are like Saturn's rings; what we love we keep as our closest ring, and what we don't want, we keep further away. And yet we are made of the whole. We can't hide from ourselves, and we surely can't hide our repressed feelings in a box somewhere far away. The greatest tool we have is self-acceptance and deep compassion which is: communion and passion. To feel passionate about our life, even in the hard times, even when we suffer in silence, for we are explorers of our own depths.

I was shown how the illusions of this reality have already been pierced through many spiritual lineages, but that it is still so hard for many people to access this wisdom because, for some reason, some find spirituality deeply intimidating; they are intimidated by the nature of their own power, laying dormant within themselves. They know that the path of spirit requires unequivocal reclaiming of one's responsibility and sovereignty for all actions, reactions, and decisions. It means addressing the source wound: our relationship to God in its Yin and Yang polarities beyond any and all dogma. And there are often inner barriers to accepting this as the victim mentality, the self-defense, and the survival mechanisms we all have within can be so immensely strong. Everything we do unto others, we do unto ourselves. Life's occurrences must be looked at from both a higher and deeper standpoint, which is easier said than done, yet it is crucial we learn how to do this.

For many, the process of awakening, or as I like to call it, self-revelation, instead of bringing peace seems to initiate so many more questions such as: why weren't we taught this in school? What does it mean about our societies? What does it mean about our culture and history? Have we been lied to? What can I truly trust, then? We need to gently allow our nervous system to soothe into spiritual self-development and, baby step by baby step, get used to this high-voltage energy passing through. We must indeed confront certain detrimental collective beliefs. For example, the belief that being a powerful, spiritually awoken individual is egotistical, which is a misinterpretation of what true divine power is. It is love manifested in a mighty, profoundly graceful way. There is a big difference between radiant power and abusive ego-centered force. True power doesn't require force. It simply beams and invites others to step into their own grace. It doesn't require being better than others and renders competition obsolete. True power simply is; it has nothing to prove.

I was shown how many people struggle to be at peace with certain experiences they went through, preventing them from fully reclaiming their sovereignty as it requires accepting that their own creative power might have led them to experience tremendous amounts of terrible, inhuman pain. Yet the threshold of crossing to the reality of self-reclamation is acceptance and objective observation as to what has been experienced. If you can learn to name it as it is, to be objective and direct, then you can soothe your deepest wounds and be reborn into your highest light. We must be willing to name things as they are, to stand in clear discernment, to confront the denial within ourselves, to un-dissociate and come back into our body.

I was then shown how humanity loves violent movies, horror and drama shows and how the lives of most humans mimics that which they consume. Some people don't understand where their nightmares come from, yet they only watch true crime shows because it's fun and they have this weird curiosity about it. Yet what is the nutritional value of what you eat, what you watch, and what you listen to? Is it really serving your well-being or peace? Be aware that what you consume, consumes you. It becomes the soundtrack, the mantra of your life. It isn't about living on a cloud somewhere far away from Earth and avoiding pop culture by all means. It's about being conscious that everything has a resonance and that we must become wise and discerning as we participate in creating the demand when it comes to what kind of entertainment, food, and services exist in the marketplace. If more people disengage from eating unhealthy processed meals, more affordable and healthy organic places will become available. If more people disengage from watching toxic entertainment, more entertainment supporting our collective well-being will be available. We set the demand.

You cannot complain about your depression, your body, or your mental health and then consume processed foods, watch violent horror entertainment, listen to life-sucking music, and expect to feel good. People do it because they feel bad, and because they feel bad, they want to consume something that will comfort how bad they feel, and so they engage in a downward spiraling loop. On the other hand, there is also the occurrence of people consuming horrifying entertainment to feel better about their lives by comparison. Strangely it awakens almost a sense of gratitude. For so long, our collective point of reference and relatability was pain. It still is in many ways, yet I set the intention through this book to shift this paradigm. Many indeed have difficulty relating to other people's successes or happiness because they haven't yet experienced it. So they feel jealous and angry. They gossip, which is the origin of sending someone the evil eye. They get bored without a sense of drama. And thus, we live in a cancel culture where we eagerly await for someone prominent to finally fail. To finally make a bad move or express a faulty or poor belief system. It feels easier to remain a martyr in our misery, for it becomes a great trick to avoid any proper action toward inner self-development. And because we are so harsh towards others, we create a collective economy of judgment and unreachable, toxic standards. That's when the little voice that says, "why is it so hard?" comes in. It is like macerating pain and turning it into this thick goo until you are paralyzed. Many creative people even believe this process is necessary for them to make good art. I would challenge anyone to question that belief. Out of respect for yourself, seek coherence within your being. If you complain about your misery and say that you seek well-being you must follow up on these words with tangible actions to support your statements, even if it's just as simple as listening to more peaceful, soothing music. You must alchemize jealousy into inspiration, your resentment, and disappointment into fuel for new.

When you live in the energy of violence, you place a big emphasis on indulgence and justification. So many people keep watching and re-watching war-oriented documentaries/shows/movies because they have deep empathy and want to educate themselves. There is a very subtle line between empathy and compassion. Empaths tend to absorb the pain of others onto themselves to their own detriment, depleting themselves of vital energy and thus being unable to help or be of support to anyone or anything as it energetically drowns them. Compassion is to sit *in passion* with someone,

.lly passionately support the person. To be present, to
y and sincerely listen, and have solidarity for our col-
lective human lives. Compassion allows us to remain strong,
connected to the light within while going deep and being of
actual qualitative support. You can imagine compassion as
your oxygen tank while going scuba diving.

Just like someone who will eat in such a way that isn't serv-
ing their health, some humans are violent because they
bypass some of the most essential spiritual laws and go
straight to a conclusion which is usually: *we're all going to
die anyway, so I might just eat this, even if it's no good for me*
or *I don't care about my energetic hygiene, I don't believe in
all that spiritual blah blah, I'll just act on whatever impulse
comes through even if I am harming myself or others.* This
is a deviation of authentic will, for our authentic will, even
if subconsciously, knows that this entire reality is made of
pure energy. We subconsciously all know this, even if we
verbally deny it. And by harming ourselves through poor
lifestyle choices, we actually engage in abuse. It might sound
harsh, but yet again this reality is profoundly detailed, and
everything has its importance, especially our daily choices
which eventually accumulate and become our lives. So many
people feel like this self-sabotage is beyond their control,
like there's an actual demon living inside of them, an in-
trusive voice that is constantly suggesting self-harm. You
must realize that your consciousness is infinite; we have all
aspects of consciousness manifesting within us: we are the
universe itself. You must tame the wild horse, tame your "in-
ner demons." You must face your shadow, bring it back into
wholeness, love it endlessly with a love so bold, so fierce,
and firm. You must use the light of truth to dismantle any
lies within you. You must cease to find excuses for giving

your power away, for these harmful self-reflections will keep bullying you into giving it away again and again. You must know it is you testing yourself. When you hear the harmful self-sabotaging voice, you must find the power from the deepest parts of yourself to say with absolute might: NO. That's what love is. You must become tremendously honest within yourself and know what is serving your well-being and what is pretending to. You must discern your absolute yes from your absolute no with immense clarity. It is easier said than done, indeed. You are a spiritual ninja in training. Discernment is a key word of immense importance. No one can teach you about discernment but direct experience. If someone tells you to believe something without any questions: run. Your discernment is your direct connection to the divine, to all information, to God itself. You must understand that these reflections of your consciousness, these so-called negative voices that are attacking you, are here to teach you something about your power. They also are part of the whole; they also are within Oneness. Our shadows can also be our greatest teachers just as much as our light.

We are the Unified Field of all experiences. The Quantum plane of all probabilities and possibilities. When you hurt yourself, you hurt others, and vice versa. Likewise, when you bless yourself, you bless others. Your actions create a ripple effect that immediately magnetizes experiences that are in the same frequency and vibration. Have you noticed how people love saying they aren't spiritual when spirit is all there is? Spirit is energy, and everything around you is energy and current. The secret is hidden in plain sight and in each word. The Current = The Voltage, the Now. The Present, the gift itself. The animating life pulsing through all that is. You need proof of God? Answer this question, where is consciousness located? You might say the brain. Yet, what is activating your brain's capacity to create perception, such as thoughts, visualization, or imagination? The most skeptical of us will say: it's simply biology. Read about it. Yet what is the animating power activating the biological body?

I was also shown the HoloDeck from Star Trek (a movie I had never seen before, but it was a clear reference given to me from the blue beings) and how everything we feel and believe creates the holographic experience around us. Our energy is essentially a toroidal field with a vortex at its center. You can imagine an apple, for example. Well, you are the point at the very middle of the apple, and your energy will create the apple's body all around you. So bringing it back to the HoloDeck analogy, you are standing in the center of an invite void. Whatever feelings, beliefs, and thoughts you generate will densify through bio-resonance into a living, breathing reality around you. It was also mentioned with tremendous importance that this holographic field is organic, it is made of light and consciousness, and it isn't what some would call a video game simulation in which we are trapped and enslaved. Yet remember: you influence the field based on the meaning you assign to it. So if you deeply believe you are a slave, your perspective will magnetize and manifest all the existing proofs in the world that this is actually the case. We are Source experiencing itself. All perspectives are valid.

Of course, I was genuinely confused. I was asking, "But how? But why? Do you mean my friends, my home, my life is a holographic illusion?" And I heard the blue beings answer me with such deep love, "Everything, absolutely everything, yes, is an illusion. But knowing that doesn't make it less special. Do you realize the love, the power that holds all these particles together for you to experience this level of detailed reality? All is a holographic illusion, including yourself. That is Maya. That is Samsara. All is a field of probabilities, quantum possibilities being magnetized to you through resonance. The only reality is that which creates the illusion itself, the vibration, the frequency, the beyond, infinity itself." Of course, I asked, "Who are you then?" And the answer I received was, "We are you, we are one. We are a direct reflection of your Higher Self, we are your guides, we aren't separate from you, and yet we are our own individuated beings. We simply vibrate on a different frequency. The frequency is established through the portal of the heart, the amount of beats per minute, per second, per instant. Your heart is the gateway to All. All beings are coordinates on the map of the multiverse." They kept sharing information with me, and I was given coordinates as to certain important dates in my family's lineage and received some very deep personal information about my grandparents I had never heard of before as my family is very private. Later on, I called my grandmother who confirmed all of it was true.

During my transcendental state, I was guided to look through a decorative crystal object my mother had gifted me for my birthday. It turns out it was a crystal lotus. Funnily enough, I had no idea of the symbolism of the lotus flower at that time and how meaningful it is in spiritual symbolism. I was instructed to look through one of the petals and into its center while placing the object at a certain angle towards the light in my room, and I saw it: infinity stretching out in its myriad colors.

Hours had passed. It was already daylight, and I had spent

the whole night writing and receiving information. My whole life after that night completely changed. In fact, I could barely go out for a couple of weeks as I felt like I could telepathically hear everything, I could hear people's stories, I could sense the future, I kept seeing visions for days. It sounds fun, but my head was exploding. I didn't want to listen or intrude on anyone's privacy as I was being given information on people that randomly passed by in the street. I had moments where it was hard for me to distinguish where I ended, and another person began, as everything felt like one unified field of consciousness. Which it is, but our human incarnation also requires boundaries. I felt like a wave moving around. Luckily I had a clairvoyant friend who held me in love and created a safe space for me to feel seen and held. I didn't need anyone's approval as I already knew what I had experienced was so real and profound, yet her care was so deeply nurturing and gave me a deep sense of validation. And then the world itself changed. In early 2020 the entire world went into lockdown. Amidst all the tremendously difficult and challenging planetary events, I actually felt deep gratitude for this synchronistic occurrence inviting our whole society to slow down and go inwards. It felt like a gift as it gave me time to integrate everything I had experienced in such a short amount of time.

I was guided to books and information that came to explain and confirm some of the things I had written in the 4 notebooks that night in 2019. I was told that my greatest gift to this world is integrity and that I must fully trust my intuition and discernment, which is how anything makes me feel in my heart and body. I was shown how I must share this, how my mission is to be a gentle, loving, compassionate, yet mighty guide for people to reconnect with their own essence, and how I would do this through music, books, social media, and much more. How my gift is in writing and that, in and of itself, this will be of profound support and assistance, knowing that those who are ready will find this book. That I mustn't be afraid in this lifetime to share this knowledge.

This book is a voyage into the depths, for the deeper you go, the higher you land: as above, so below. And at the core of your being, there is a fountain: the experience of your own divinity. Words can guide you to it, like a symphony, a river moving you gently. Some might want to swim against the current, yet if you relax into the stream, you will be brought to the destination you seek. You'll get it. There was and is nothing to seek, for it was and is always here, hidden in plain sight. Who hid it? Yourself a long time ago. And yet as time and space don't actually exist for you essentially are the zero still point of all: there is an experience that you chose as the eternal consciousness you are to forget what you are and enjoy the fun of remembering it again. I know how mind-boggling that sounds. The best metaphor I can share to illustrate this is: there was a time I used to hide little notes or dried flowers between the pages of some of my favorite books. Oh, what a joy it would bring me to forget I had hidden it there and simply one day find it again. You are eternal, infinite nature. Of course, you will explore your creative resourcefulness. There is no place to go, no place to be, for your destination is here and now, beating at the center of your heart. That consciousness of who you were before you were born, that spaciousness, that void, the womb of the great Mother holding you, the light of the great Father enlightening you, your cosmic family re-parenting you to your own Sovereign self-recognition.

It has been said in many spiritual traditions that God has 72 names. And for that, there are 72 poems, prayers, or incantations in this book. Many concepts are repeated as our minds learn a great deal through repetition. It is intended that certain formulations are mentioned several times. Call them as you wish; they are here to re-activate the memory of who you are. Remember the Mystery. There are 7 portals or gateways lifting the 7 veils of Illusion. Walk in surrender, remembrance, revelation, purification, activation, integration and bliss.

To you, dear seeker, what you are looking for is already here in the palms of your wise hands. Let the loving light of wisdom ignite your burning heart from within and re-activate all of you as the warrior of light, a warrior fighting without weapons but with compassion, wisdom and love. Find here what you need and go forth rejoicing in your victory as the brave one who chose to meet itself.

Sincerely,
To You
To Me
To We
To Thee
As One.

Kristina

GUIDELINES

☽ ✻ ☾

You may read this book in any way that feels appropriate. From beginning to end, from end to beginning, by simply opening it up at a random page and seeing what message shows up for you today. This book is an oracle and can be used like a tarot deck. If reading for the first time, I highly suggest reading it from start to finish to really integrate each activation, as each portal is an initiation in and of itself.

You may then read it to yourself or to others, to your inner child or your actual children, to your partner, your family members, and friends. You can read the poems aloud like invocations. You can use them like prayers to activate and bless your water, your food, and cleanse your space. You can chant it into the fire, into the wind, into the ocean as an offering.

You can sing the words, whisper them, and speak them aloud or silently in your mind. Whatever you feel is right is the way. Whatever feels good is the way. Whatever brings you joy is the way.

Let the miracles of these poems speak and resonate in your heart; let them guide you on your path of remembrance, acceptance, and integration. You're coming back home to being All of You. Being the Realized One and aligning with your highest, deepest potential, aware of your Essence. Actually experiencing it physically.

May each page come to life as you read it. May you use these words in meditation or during New Moon/Full Moon ceremonies. May you offer these symphonies to Earth while out in a forest or field. May you read them gently before going to bed and let them beam through your consciousness as gems, treasures of your own creation that brought you here in this divine synchronicity. Whenever you need guidance: just know they are here. They found themselves to you as you found your way to yourself.

IN - CAN - TARE

THE ART FORM OF
PRONOUNCING INCANTATIONS.

TO CHANT A NEW REALITY INTO LIFE.

TABLE OF CONTENTS

☽ ☼ ☾

SURRENDER

FIREWALL ORDER

DECLARATION————

I Am divine presence and I am One
With the divine presence of God

As one Consciousness, One Field
One breath, One Voice, One Heartbeat

I accept myself as I Am, Entirely
I now choose to see myself in my totality
I hereby decree, affirm and confirm
Energetically Order and Absolutely Command
That any and all victimhood, self-harm
self-sabotage, denigrating, abusive, intrusive
corrupted, corruptive thoughts, patterns
Beliefs, ideas, programs, inner and outer systems
Be now, immediately as I decree
Seen, Revealed, Acknowledged
Accepted, Dismantled, and Loved back into Wholeness
Cleansed and Purified by the Power of
Source's loving Light with whom I am One
Filtered and Re-arranged by

An All Consuming Violet Fire
Within and all around me
Assisting me continuously
In all ways, always and at all times
I allow my inner light

The central sun of my Being
To beam through any and all:

Lies, denial and anything detrimental to me
This happens beyond the speed of my thoughts
As I read and pronounce this I simply know
This happens effortlessly and beyond logic
For my deepest well-being and highest good
As well as the most wholesome peace of all
I am the Universe's Creativity in Action.

It is so.

THE DIAMOND

I stand in the center of a Diamond
Of Adamantine Grace
Each facet beaming the many Faces
The many Names of Creation itself

Divine Wisdom
Divine Truth
Divine Love

Three Orbs guarding
Perfection

All is your projection
And all is a reflection
For the source of creation
Is at the center of your heart

The center is at the center of each star
And you, my dear, are made of stardust
A body of galaxies shining from afar

I see bright Roses enveloping me
As a current of bliss stretches my spine
And a tender voice whispers gently:
Follow the Middle Line
There you will see the holy Shrine

The Union of Black and White
The Union of Feminine and Masculine
The Union of Empty and Plenty
The Union of Inhale and Exhale
The path is the Spine.
The Union is within.
The path is Ascension.

COMMUNION

Sitting here in Divine Communion
In absolute Union with All
I recognize:

I Am One within Oneness
And Oneness within One

I am Peace
I am Whole
I am Infinity

My Spirit is Eternal
My Soul is Immortal
My love is the Portal
Between Worlds

Horus, The Eye of Horus
Is rising from my Love
I am Infinite Wealth
I am Infinite Health
All the chemistry
Exists Within me

For I am the Unified Field itself
Where Miracles and Sacred Healings Manifest
I am the Ocean of Consciousness itself
The drop in the water, the water in the drop

Horus, The Eye of Horus.
I now See.

RELATIVITY

How do you take? How do you breathe in?
How do you express receptivity?
How is your taste for victory?
Do you welcome it effortlessly?
Or do you rip off out of desperation, need, and greed?
From the inner well, everything comes gently.

How do you give? How do you exhale?
How do you express generosity?
What is your tone of authenticity?
Do you share? With deep care?
Or do you save up all your energy
thinking that is the fate of your destiny?

For how you give is how you receive.

The quality of your inhale reflects
the depth of your exhale.

The inner fountain within you
Has no pennies to count
It is the ever-pouring
Sustainable Source
Overflowing with treasures
And blessings to be found
The inner well you shall find
And you will see there:
All bounty abounds.

AWARENESS

I be and come aware
Of the Space that sees
With my eyes closed
The space that dreams
When I drift off

This space called imagination
A myriad of images and nations
So real and tangible yet
Made of particles of light
Surging through me

I be and come aware
Of that space

The eyes behind my eyes
The sight behind my sight

I now, become.

RADIANCE

My boundaries are firm
They Reflect Light

Only crystal clear love is allowed in
For my glorious Delight

Any and all lies, denial or abuse
Can no longer subside
Within and Without
My fire ignites.
I dwell in bliss
And declare:
So it is.

ALCHEMY

In the Resonance of the Absolute
The Ever Present, Everlasting
Union of All Particles, Gems of Light
All Visible and Invisible Realities
All Pathways and All Realms
My Dear Holy, Wholly Infinity
I Recognize you, We Are One
I am the Path and I am the Way
The Adventure and the Adventurer
And forever so always.

I am the Space and Time Continuum
Experiencing itself in its vastness
I am the flame, the burning love
Piercing throughout any and all denial
I choose to let go of any and all stories
To see beyond the Beyond
The spark that ignited the Passion
The Cosmic Dance
That Birthed the Whole

I am the Space and the Spaces in Between
The very Tapestry itself
Made of all the colors and more
I am made of swirling waves of dancing sounds
And a river or sparkling igniting stars

The Mysterious.
I know it at Heart.
Without ever being able to put it into words

For it cannot be contained or laid on paper
For it has always been adorned in layers
So I transform the weight of density
Into a subtler form of chemistry
In the cauldron of my art.

I now choose to truly see
I now choose to truly Be
I now choose Infinity
I am, We are, Stars

I now choose to access the core of my being
To become aware of my Essence
And Sovereign of my Presence

To bring myself back into Wholeness
To love myself as Greatness
To reveal myself, to Myself: in my totality
To surrender to my immortality

To peak at Eternity
And let myself dive into Bliss
Igniting in Awe within a sacred Kiss

I realize: I am my divine purpose
Within the purity of my pose I stand
Rejoicing on this wild Journey
As I allow this inner Alchemy

DEVOTION

My Voice is my Sword
My Step is my Stone
My Heart is my Throne

THE GIFT

Give yourself the gift of your sacred Presence
Pause and Reflect for a bit
Our minds always try to find solutions
Yet our hearts knew it this whole time
Can you hear the gentle quiet voice of your heart
In the Tumult?

Can you listen with your inner ears?
What if the solution isn't outside
But inside of you?

In the darkest and most hidden places
where you hid yourself
From yourself
To protect yourself
And then you barricaded yourself
Out of your own Love

What if silence could bring you gently to the shores
Of your own meeting
And Inspiration

In the stillness of your soul resides all the knowledge
All the records of the known and unknown
Allow yourself to feel it
And once you are ready
You shall receive the gift

MATTER

You ask what love is?

Love takes many forms, and yet it is formless
It is a current boundless to time
A language heard by the soul both
the bird and the elephant understand

Love isn't a feeling or emotion
It's a state, and that which holds
All particles together
Love is a divine chemistry
Drawing the very lines of reality
It is subjective and objective
It emerges from the center

Love is deep trust in unlimited creation
I trust you means I may surrender in your arms
Like falling in a bed of feathers
Safe and Sound
Always Home

For that is what Source is
When flowing Unobstructed
Throughout you
It simply wants to express and be
It wants to dance and chant
So you may ask what love is
It is simply You
And it is simply Me

☽ ✧ ☾

To all those carrying the wound of rejection
The witch wound, the silencing of one's miracle work

The Yin brings us in, in the infinite darkness of the
Nothingness. The Yang manifests into form, light
becomes structured Creation: the Everything.

In ancient times wise men and wise women
were the beholders of lightwork and miracles.
They worked with plants and mighty chants to
heal their people. They told stories about the
Great Spirit and the mysteries of this world.

They were then called witches and wizards and deemed
profane. Yet, how is spellwork different from prayer?
Words can be both used to hurt and to heal
The root of it all is sacred intention

Preaching in the name of God, when done from a place
of greed and hate, can cause just as much harm as magic.
Both can be used for good or evil deeds. Both work with
spirit, with energy, with the invisible realms of this reality.

May your divine discernment guide you as you proceed.

GRID

For the blood we shed
For the wisdom that burned
The many faces lost in the fires
So many we tried to erase
from the surface of the Earth
Came back even stronger
Never forgotten, oh no
For energy can never die
It can only be transformed
Mutating in the ethers, becoming
Even wiser, even bolder

The blood flowing out of Women
The mighty river many consider
Punishment for Eve's mistake
For her biting into knowledge
We reclaim this flow we make
And we offer it onto the soil
On a moonlit night, glowing skin
We offer it back onto the Land
For all that has been felt
And all that has led
To this very moment

And the witch is now that which is so deeply needed
The wise men and women are now coming forward
And activating the sacred pathways of the Earth
The intelligent Grids and all of its Geometry
They are known as ley lines, the mighty keys

The Children of the Stars have descended
of their own Will to Dance here again
To re-awaken the Cynical minds living in
denial, draped in their capes of arrogance
The ones that live in austerity, the ones sac-
rificing their will to cynicism and pity

They will be forgiven, for we are liberating all.
We now liberate ourselves fully

The Seeds of Light are here to re-awaken the lost knowledge
They sing: you have the Power within.
Know that you are:
Re-membered

—PORTAL 2—

REMEMBRANCE

BALANCE

I invoke my sacred balance from within
I invoke my sacred essence from within
I align with unconditional grace and faith
To my perfect peace and coherence
I walk on the brilliant thread of life
In divine equilibrium with cosmic law

Manifest and Un-manifest
At Peace with it All

I am gentle, light as a feather, in harmony with
Air, Fire, Water, and Earth, wise Elements of Gaia
Carrying me throughout this Human Incantation
Multidimensional Incarnation

Mighty Earth. Thank you for building my body.
Thank you for lending it to me, for this time.

From within I am centered
Aligned and synchronized
Within the Expanded Self, I am
A flower of life, a lotus of infinite colors
My petals blooming as morning dew
My True Sight is kaleidoscopic
My heartbeat deliciously ecstatic

As I surrender, I allow the divine flow of Grace to
Balance all parts of my being on all levels

Thank you for this blessed re-alignment.
And for my capacity to sustain coherence
Within my body, spirit, and integrity
I am whole. I am Now and all is well.

PERFECTION

I am Perfect
Not as a Result
But as that which any Result
Can occur through
I am an Instrument
Of the Divine

The Colors of the Cosmos painting me
The music of the Stars singing me
I am the Everything and Nothing
The eternal, the unspeakable.
Words shiver at my sight
In reverence and delight
I am both silence and sound
The still point and the wave
The first light after darkness
The spark
The One.

GHOST

People are scared of hungry ghosts at midnight's hour
And were told their darkness is "bad" and unholy
So they put all their garbage, all their judgements
All their guilt, blame, terror and shame in a box
Lock it up and seal it somewhere far, far away

And then in the loneliest hour's peak
When the cosmic mother reveals all ills
One can hear a howling drill

The mirror that is life magnetizes
Situations for deep cellular liberation
The box's contents are revealed again

Hungry Ghosts are your projections
Your inner detrimental self reflections
How blessed you are to see them
Welcome them in your arms and
Thank them for making you aware
Of where you long for recognition
Your hungry ghosts are your pointers
Indicating you where your cracks are

That inner child that cried at night
Saw visions in its dreams that felt so true
That little one is you, it stopped because
It was told "that's not what humans do"
The child just heard: I don't believe you
What you feel, what you see isn't true
So then the hungry ghost appeared again

Crying:

Let me dream
Let me feel
Let me be

The hungry ghost is the sadness we repress
The hungry ghost is the child we oppress
The hungry ghost is all the joy we forbid
The Ghosts will disappear once you recognize
And make it clear:

The Universe lives in you.
You are it, and it is you.
Yes, you see, yes you are:
Miraculous Nature itself.
Your inner world so true.
You are a sacred channel
Your visions are honored.

Denial can no longer abide
Abuse can no longer subside
No matter what it takes
It is time to choose embrace
Feel what you must feel
Let it move through you
And in that moment the ghost will reveal
Itself to you, as the being it always was:
A fragment of you
That which you hid in that box
And deemed as bad
Making yourself wrong
Even if just one part

The part is the whole
And the whole is the part
It is time to bring yourself home
And leave no trace
No abandoned face
The hungry ghost turns then into
An angel of light
Guarding
Protecting
And blessing you.

RISING

We humans try to understand everything logically
And yet when we dive into our hearts we can feel
The absolute delightfulness of the emptiness itself
This regenerative space where all possibilities reside
So what are we trying to grasp or understand?
What are we trying to stand under?

I invite you to Inner Stand.
I invite us to Inner Rise.

I Inner Rise to my delight in simply Being
I Inner Rise to my Joy of being a Creator
I Inner Rise to my most wholesome well-being
Thriving in All ways, Always and at all times
In absolute divine respect of all.

In the ordinary, I find the extraordinary
I gently observe my imagination,
How it composes itself etherically
Behind the curtain of my closed eyes

In the infinite space between my eyebrows
There the whole rainbow resides

I Bring back all my Members home
Yes I Re-member
Back in my body
Aware

A deep knowing that never truly left
It simply got shadowed by stories
A choosing to forget, memories buried deep
Forgetting the very choice of this amnesia itself
And the coming to this very moment of awareness
Finding me again, like a treasure hunt with self
To retrieve all my ancient memories
And recognize this eternal mystery

I now Rise.

CLARITY

Do you seek outside of yourself
The validation and approval you ought
to find inside of yourself?

What is external reality but
a projection of an inner mentality?

Life is always going to mirror you
both your doubts and certainties.
So choose accordingly

You are valid for you are.
Make no mistake.
There is nothing to prove.
Nothing to take.

Who can actually validate your talent,
worth, and beauty other than yourself?
We let others love us to the degree
that we allow ourselves to Love

Have a hard time being convinced of your own worth?

Well instead of convincing, try:
Self-approving and respecting.
Try deep inner honesty.
Don't even try: simply be.
That's beautiful enough.
You are immeasurably enough.
You are a unique composition.

Reflect on your inner disposition.
You are beyond any and all measures.
You are a pure unique symphony.

You are.
And that's enough.

LOVE

We often say to "fall in love"
Yet are you really falling?
Can you rather rise in love?
Can you rather stand in love?

Can you rather make love your unconditional foundation?

We often think of love as something romantic
Worth suffering for
Can you rather ground in love?
So deeply that these roots nurture your whole being
Can you rather see how you are made of this mighty sap
Can you let it pour throughout you entirely?

We often say love hurts.
Yet can we rather think of love as that which
enables any and all experiences?
Like the very gravity itself holding all things in place
Like the glue, the goo pulling matter together

We often speak of love as something to believe in or not
Yet can we rather think of it as the very

Absolute?

RECEPTIVITY

I accept letting go of the old
To welcome in the new

I am space
I am empty
I am plenty

Both Infinite, Both One

I release that which no longer serves me
That which feels stagnant and outgrown
Anything that feels:

Shameful
Harmful
Stressful
All that is full
Has no room
No space

For me to expand
For me to be
And express freely

I now allow Source's Loving Light
This unconditional radiance
To cleanse me fully
Like a waterfall
A crystalline curtain
Adorning me

I now find Real Ease.

I open to Receive
This blessing.

I step into the unknown
For I know that is where miracles happen
No longer bound to pre-conceived
Or limited ideas of Reality

All is Now
I am Now
The Present
The Gift

I am depth and receptivity

I am

THE WOMB

I pray upon the morning star
Guiding me always to heal my scars
I pray upon the dove of innocence
Innocence that can never be lost
Or broken, for it is at the very core
Of an unbreakable space
Made of un-shattering lace

A liquid light
Emerging from the depths
Of Nothingness
Bathing me in
Remembrance
A cellular activation
A dream within a dream

A darkness so warm and good
We have forgotten it is the womb
Of the Great Cosmic Mother
As the multi-colored Rays
Of the Cosmic Father
Exist simultaneously

A darkness we have confused with shadow
For shadow creates an obstacle to light
Yet darkness is the space holding the whole
As the calm sun within it ignites

I reconcile with the power of prayer
I reconcile with the word God & Goddess
I reconcile with Bounty, Wealth and Prosperity
For that is Who and What I truly am.

Beyond dogma and Belief.
I Be and I live.
Simply and beautifully.
In the Womb of Infinity.

—PORTAL 3—

REVELATION

ALONENESS

When you look closely into Aloneness
There you will find Oneness

It is safe to be All One
For Alone you never really Are
Your inner exalted, expanded being
Rejoices in the quality presence you give yourself
Love is eventually how you allow others to love you
And how you allow yourself to love others

All is divine reflection
Dancing through the fluid curtain of holographic reality
Remember: all is a lucid dream in Matter
Cells aren't a prison, your mind isn't confined
You are inherently free
Your body is a temple:

It is sacred
Speak to it
It listens

Just like you can hear the ripples of the rain
So can each particle surrounding you
Speak to them
They hear you
Ask for guidance and signs
Feel into it
And believe, Be and Live the answers themselves

The fluid, the flow always listens and it will
always respond in a loving whisper

REFLECTION

Darkness is a simple
Reflection of Light
Casting and Manifesting in
Form and Shape for your senses to witness
The Contrasts of this Physical Reality

Yet shadow is an obstacle to light
It hides and dissimulates
What your mind can't assimilate

The whole Holographic field
Is a dancing of many light shields
Boundaries or none being expressed
Octaves of sound being impressed

Honor the edges, honor the boundaries and the thorns
Of this world. Honor the contrasts of this present Reality

You came here for this expression
To see the Holiness of Matter and feel
how energy translates into it

Your body vehicle is here to explore your one Infinite body
throughout this Time and Space modality
This divine dichotomy is inviting you
To acknowledge Oneness even in the seeming appearance
Of Duality itself

Unique in our Togetherness

You are in the living Belly of your own divine nature
You aren't even born yet
You are in the sacred womb of Earth
Waiting to be reborn anew
Into your Eternity

COMPASS

There are many worlds inside of you
Many roads to be explored
eventually all lead to the same place
As the Roots reflect the branches

Those you meet on your path are reflections
Mirroring all the ways life may express
Itself on the infinite path
This Tantric Motion at Play

Remember All is One, all is You
You may seem to move yet
You are the absolute stillness
You may think you came here to learn
Yet what is there to learn
When you are ever present
Everlasting wisdom itself
Creating this experience
For you to play in?
The origin of all worlds
The essence of all intelligence itself
Manifesting in all forms
You may seem to move yet
In the quantum body you are
always still

Yet forever expanding
As simultaneously, Source
Explores itself as You

There is nothing to accomplish
Nothing to do for all is done
All is space, moving and still
You are traveling through You
And simultaneously just know this:

All is yet to be done too.

So unveil your deepest wishes
For they are already created
They are already here in you

You are thy Lighthouse
The emanating light
The trust guiding you ashore
The thunder and the sparkling flame

You are water, limpid and fluid
Always dancing within the rain

Follow thy compass and know that you are always
At the right place and at the right time
You're never missing out when
you let the great awareness guide you
Let your clearest joy lead your way ahead

And in the hardest days know
The harshest storms
Water many flowers
Your love is your pass.

THE 7 RAYS

To the Seven Dancing Sisters in the Sky
The Pleiadian Starcodes
Pulling us ever up high

To the seven days of week
To the seven rays within
Lifting tenderly the seven veils herein
Illusions so subtle, so thin
Yet they can trouble you
lead you to forget thy real Kin

The first ray of Ruby Bright
A Garden of Roses Blooming in Delight
A Queen of Hearts holds her Sword
Dismantles her own Greed
And renders her Soil
Fertile with Holy Seeds

The second ray of Copper Haze
Where many Kings got lost in a deadly Maze
Of their own inner conflicts and most terrible days
Yet once they recognize the Maze is of their own Making
A hidden Door suddenly appears

The third ray: The Golden Gate
The Portal to all Suns in The Universe
Alcyone, Helios, & Vesta
Dancing in the Sky, The Door of Victory
The Next Ray will bring you Closer
To the One

The fourth ray of Green Emerald sky
A love so deep there is no asking Why
A Temple of Birth where all Questions are
Answered before they even arise
A sanctuary of Truth
Where abides no Lie

The fifth ray of Powder Blue shade
An expression of Depth that can never wade
A Crystal of Light that can never fade
The Voice of Angels bursting awake
The Creative Word
Sealing Thy Fate

The sixth ray of Indigo Light
Elevating you above the darkest clouds
And the phantoms of the night
There your true vision arises
And ablaze it suffices
To ignite all the Storms
In the Womb of the All
There you were Born

The seventh ray of Deep Purple Hue
There you recognize God, Goddess is You
And we are One as we always were
The Source of Eternity
That always Unfolds

You now wear your Crown
And honor your Throne.
As the mighty one
You succeed

Your mission is done.

There the 7 Sisters of All Universes Dance
As the Elohims lift all beings from trance
Their own dreams and illusions
The silly games and stubborn ideas
Keeping them away from recognizing
The Miracle of their very Existence

There the Arcturian Brothers join us all to play
Sealing all Tunnels without any delay
The wheel of Incarnation is done
All Masks are now Gone
When all beings realize

What is real with their inner eyes.

BOUNTY

All Resources Flow To Me
From Source Directly
I abound in Bounty

I choose to Receive
And get out of my own way
I open myself up truly
To my infinite abundance
Blessing me in all ways

I choose to bless others
Through my Service
And Genuine Grace
For I weave prosperity
In every single place

Yes I know, I am truly rich
In so many genuine ways

I bask in my resourcefulness
And I now see: I am bounty
I am the mighty Tree

TRANSPARENCY

The Universe, Multi-Verse, The One Great All
The Absolute, God, Goddess, Infinity
Sees and Knows All of Me

I Orient the Course of my Adventure through
Each Choice, Each Word, Each Thought

Abracadabra

I create as I speak

My attention energizes my Will
My Intention magnetizes and transforms my Reality

I am a Creator, a Master Manifestor
I let go of the Hero and Villain archetypes
For I see how it's a codependent dichotomy
That coexists in the Dual game within me
I acknowledge that in the gameplay of
The victim and abuser, both coincide
For both gave their power away

As one forgot its power
Of a Whole Hearted Yes
And a Whole Hearted No

The other forgot that he is in all
Experiencing its very own self
Abusing therefore of his very own essence
Forgetting its own deeply sacred Presence

The Hero and Villain exist
Co-Dependently
When there is nothing to save
And nothing to break
The Hero and the Villain both vanish
Then codependency shifts into:

Inter-reality

Co-Creative Synergy
Indeed

The Universe sees and knows all of me.

The Universe sees and knows all my desires, all my wishes
And I hereby orient and sail my boat
to the shores of my inner

Heaven on Earth

Heaven on Earth is simply a frequency
Like a radio station, on a specific channel of
Crystal Clear Clarity
Absolute Transparency
A State, an Island: it Is The Land
Already existing within me
To access it I simply release denial
Transfigure the Veils of my Shadow Identity
Hiding Me away from me
From the truth of All Reality

I unveil myself now.

I acknowledge that I have chosen
in the past to play a game
Where I hid myself away from me, a cosmic hide and seek
For the thrill and appreciation of finding me again
In my infinite eternity.
I choose now a new game.
The one of love beaming Seamlessly

OCEAN OF SOUND

☽ ✿ ☾

There's a difference between bypassing negative thoughts, meaning ignoring them, and simply not feeding/macerating/indulging in them. The question is often, what do you feed within? What do you give power to within? How do you nurture yourself? That which you give power to grows. The grass is green where you water it, you see. Indeed we often ask ourselves, why do negative thoughts even appear? They show up from duality, and duality is how we perceive contrasts and oppositions.

When we remember Oneness, that we are One within Oneness and Oneness within One, we may recognize that these thoughts are just passing through, like a wave in the Ocean of Consciousness. You aren't just the wave. You are the whole Ocean itself. You aren't your thoughts. You are the space allowing them to arise and be witnessed. We may choose to recognize that it's a stream, a seamless flow. In the Ocean of all thoughts, you are the Observer, and when you attach or identify yourself to a thought, it's like you click and press play on its movie. Do you invest in the worst-case or best-case scenarios? Most invest in worst-case scenarios because they feel more "realistic" and more "relatable," like these sad indie movies that we all used to love as teenagers. Because many still identify themselves as victims and that life is punishing them, it seems like a modest yet honorable role to portray. So they keep investing more into it mentally/emotionally/energetically, comforting their ills and thus creating more of that reality. Pain becomes an identity. And that is the secret lock of a hero/villain mentality.

Many try to escape a punishment they secretly believe they deserve. They let guilt operate their life. Yet understand this: it is the program of guilt running on your mind that manifests the reality of a fault itself. Read that again. Because we let guilt occupy so much of our inner mental space, thinking it is the primary tool of our moral compass when it's not, we create lack and disappointment, which are both manifestations of original guilt. Guilt makes you doubt your own will and creative power like you could have always done better. Like you're never enough. Your wisdom is your safest discernment tool, not guilt. Wisdom will always bring you where you wish to go, not guilt. Wisdom will assist you in respecting yourself and others. Guilt will block you, isolate you, and paralyze you. So again, I ask: what do you allow to dominate your inner mental space? If you let your inner "demons" run around freely inside your mental space without ever taming them, it is like opening the doors of your apartment and letting the most disrespectful individuals roam around your place and leave trash everywhere with no consideration for your well-being. That's what happens when you allow or are internally bullied into letting these inner critics, inner abusers, dominate your inner space. We talk about boundaries, well, realize that inner boundaries are extra important. Energy hygiene and energy management are everything. You must tame your inner critic, tame the voice of arrogance, tame the voice of the detrimental abusive perfectionist, tame the voice of dissatisfaction, the condescending nagging voice. Tame them. Don't let them dominate you. You are the boss of your inner space. Take your power back and be fierce.

You can do this.

We may practice and see it with clarity: these hurtful, fearful thoughts, are they serving me? Are they useful? Are they preventative? Or are they paralyzing me? Blocking me and my potential? Do I benefit from being paralyzed because I don't know where I want to go? What benefits do I get from this self-sabotage?

Say: I may now rewrite my story. I firmly choose to be well and happy and align all my actions to this radical statement, whatever it takes. I choose clarity and wisdom guiding me from within, I choose to become consciously aware of my most wholesome discernment always leading me, guiding me towards my most authentic well-being.

I recognize Source is Love, not the romantic kind of Love we know of. The unspeakable, grand Love, the Essence of All. The Unlimited Creativity present within All. That is the Ultimate Truth known by many Yogis. Then as different planes of form appear within the infinite ocean of consciousness, there is a possibility to explore with contrasts and polarities. There is nothing "wrong" with polarities, nothing "wrong" with Samsara: it allows a spectrum of experiences. We are here to express our mastery, to practice the impeccable balance of Yin and Yang, of Doing and Being, The 0 & the 1, The Passive and Active, The Projector and The Receptor, The + & -, the Cosmic battery, the Taurus shape of Existence with the Vortex of Creation itself. Recognizing our Oneness with all, truly being an alchemist of feelings and emotions, allowing this energy in motion to move without blocking it is what fulfillment is. Being healthy is keeping our channels and our inner pipes clear and flowing. People wish to be psychic: this is how you do it. Simply allow your inner Omniscient,

Expanded, and Wholly (whole + holy) self to guide you. Recognizing our "lower" self isn't bad; it's part of the whole. This human experience isn't just about the Higher Self. It's about the expanded self. It's about integrity. High and low are simply placements on a scale of cosmic music. Source allows in neutrality for all experiences without judging. You are in your Whole Self. Just like sound, like octaves on an infinite cosmic piano whose melody is heard throughout the eternal frequency spectrum of God, the inner I Am presence. A lower note isn't "bad" compared to a higher note; in fact, usually in a harmonious symphony, bass notes accompany high notes. The left side or moon/feminine side of the body plays the bass notes, and the right, sun/masculine side of the body plays the higher notes. It's a reflection of the dark womb of the Cosmic Mother and the light rays of the Cosmic Father. We are this Love. We are Music. We are Symphonies, Ever-Present Melodies.

Let's remember each and every second that there is absolutely no separation between us and the Divine. We are It. You must feel it, not just understand it theoretically. For if you stand under this wisdom, you simply miss it. Really feel into it. You are each particle of this Holographic Field. And this Holographic Field is organic, it's a fractal symphony of Nature's Beauty and Bounty. Where the whole is in the One, and the One is in the Whole. Let flowers, rivers and trees teach you this. Let a bird show you this. Let the ripples of a stone on water guide you into this wisdom. Tune into this vibrationally. Let your inner child play. The inner child who always knew miracles and magic are real and saw dragons in the sky. Sense this with your whole body, *YOU ARE.* You are Absolute. Perfect Love. Perfect peace, Perfect space.

Say it with me :

I settle firmly in All the Love I am. I allow myself to connect to the deepest, crystalline clarity and honesty within me. I am. I reveal All of Me to Me and real-ease shame and blame as I accept and love even these parts of me. I am Wholly. I am Whole and Holy. With so much compassion for all of me. I allow myself to reflect on that which needs to come up now so that I may bring all of me back into wholeness by the power of my awareness and see myself in my totality. I let my heart guide the way. My heart is mighty. I choose ever-present, ever-lasting Transparency with a capital T. I allow myself to feel all the Gratitude I Am as I surrender into this eternal now. I am both the eternal Stillness and the eternal Movement. I am both frequency and vibration. I am both form and formless.

You might now ask: what are then these seeming moments of ungratefulness? What are they trying to tell me ? These moments are like "falling" into amnesia again of one's own true nature. Willingly choosing to experience the opposite of one's own greatness which in fact doesn't exist. It doesn't exist because it suffers. Existing, truly existing and suffering cancel each other out. You cannot exist and suffer. When you suffer you feel dead within, thinking Source left you, that you are separate from it, separate from yourself, or that God is punishing you. You believe you are separate from all that is good, that you never asked for this life. So ungratefulness appears when you aren't truly present. It appears when you dissociate or leave your body. That is why the ones who suffer, who feel ungrateful are ones who feel dead and morbid inside. Compassion my dear one, we've all been there and all go through these spaces eventually. Oftentimes it is so because we secretly miss the dark womb of the Mother. We miss being in her belly as un-manifested creatures. We miss having no response-ability. So we get angry at incarnation, at density and wish upon destruction of all matter. One who macerates its suffering often isn't in its body, it's floating above it and feeding on toxic energy to validate its pain. Its body is vacant and so it's temporarily soulless, the soul is floating somewhere else, oftentimes in fragments. Yet this is never permanent and is allowed as an experience on your adventure of energy mastery. The great mother indeed allows all experiences for her children to learn. And this too is love and is beautiful. Even the soulless instants have a spark within.

The great mother wasn't able to protect its own children from their own pain: she had to allow them to experience the full spectrum of all that is. That is how generous and permissive the universe is. It doesn't lock its emanations into safety bubbles, it lets its children on a wild and raw self exploration: a true energetic scavenger hunt. The Divine Mother, The Divine Father live within You. Ingratitude sees all life as unfair, as a punishment. It sees the experience of being in a human body like being trapped in a cage and death being the only issue. That is why it doesn't exist. For when you exist you feel and are fully alive which comes automatically with gratefulness because you see the cosmic tapestry and the grandeur of this physical reality that manifested from literally nothing. Do you see the subtle difference? The one who suffers is in conflict with it's very own nature. The only way out of pain is conscious re-connection to oneness.

Let's make an analogy: imagine ski slopes and pathways

being drawn in a thick layer of fresh snow. The weight of the skier creates a trail in the shimmering duvet of ice. Your neural pathways are similar. When you are used to thinking a certain way, you create a trail in your nervous system. That is called a pathway. Or a pattern. And it is quite convenient to follow the same pathway on and on as the markers on the snow become heavier and heavier, more and more drawn in. Until you realize and ask yourself: is this pathway serving me? So the one who suffers must find the key out of its own cage and recognize its response-ability. Its ability to respond and create. The path of forgiveness is the path of liberation. You aren't forgiving someone who harmed you and condoning ill will. You are for-giving and offering yourself the greatest gift: liberation.

By recognizing, appreciating, and accepting your ability to create a vast spectrum of experiences, including great suffering, you realize that is how free and sovereign you are and that is how generous and trusting the Universe is. For if the Universe feared you'd mess this whole thing up, it wouldn't have allowed you to embody. You can't mess this up. Experience is experience.

The path of loving your own creation is for-giving. You *give* naturally *for* experience to occur. Giving yourself many varied experiences for your soul's energetic self mastery. For when you forgive yourself for all the monsters and demons you faced on your quest, even if at times you failed the battles, the adventure becomes fun again. The quest was never intended for the faint of heart. You came here for intensity. You are an adventurer. You came here for a ride and the most immersive and "realistic" experience possible, one so intense it could make you forget that you are Source air dropping to experience itself. Now when you awaken, you can choose if you wish more gentleness, serenity and calm by creating new pathways and using your response - ability in innovative manners. How much love can you allow without feeling guilt? How much love can you allow until shame comes to tickle you? When you rise, do you let others rise alongside you or do you wish to rise to be above others? These are greatly important questions and you will be tested by your own expanded self in order to answer them through your choices and radical self affirming actions.

Is your only way of having fun to be better than others and compete? Is your only way of fun to go against the grain and make yourself seem different from everyone: thus constantly playing the role of the outsider as your only means of feeling special? Can you accept all the love that you are without wanting to be better than others or seek revenge for the pain you went through? Can you accept success without the need to avenge your childhood traumas? These are all your tests. Who's testing you? Yourself.

When you are fully IN your body and not floating above trying to escape this incarnation, or as some might interpret it: incarceration, remind yourself to come back in the body. Again and again. Your body is miraculous. It truly is. When you are fully IN your body and not floating above it, know that you are One with All. Your body sends you vital information as to where you are located energetically and what you must become aware of and alchemize in yourself: this can indeed be uncomfortable. Yet your body is the portal, it is wisdom itself. When you are in your body fully: you spark, you truly glimmer for you come to life and that optimizes your magnetic field and life becomes miraculous. If you are floating above it, ask yourself what are you trying to avoid, what are you seemingly trying to protect yourself from? If you aren't in your body because you dissociate from it just know: you add more gasoline into the fire, meaning, you make the situation in some ways worse, even if it feels necessary or even the only way for you to survive. When you dissociate from your body you basically leave it vacant, you don't occupy your space. And that's when psychic possessions and attacks might occur. You might not even realize it but suddenly you have a roommate as you left your body vacant for so long: there is the shadow of yourself. Don't freak out, just remind yourself of the one principle repeated in this book over and over again: all is one. So this "inner roommate" is a reflection of your own feeling of being lost and looking for a home. Sometimes when we experience trauma, we fragment and we dissociate from the now to continuously contemplate a wound from afar. Yet deeply, fully, and totally feeling the wound in the body and letting the emotions move as they need to in radical self compassion and acceptance is the only way to release them: to bring real ease.

When we lose someone we love we feel lack, absence and abandonment. The abandonment wound is so present in so many of us. The loss of a relationship, the departure of a friend. A mourning, grief. Yet energy never dies, it only transforms. In this realm we can never truly possess anything. So how can you grasp onto something or someone? How can you say life is too short when you might not even be living it fully? As you embody wholeness, you become embodied Oneness experiencing itself and you just know that nothing is ever lost or gone. When you live each moment fully you accept the natural shedding of skin. You accept life's cycles. Reality is ever shifting, merging and moving. The one who left an incarnation was merely our reflection in space/time. The timing is always correct in the field of all probabilities. Would you mourn your friend the caterpillar if it transformed into a butterfly before you did? Death of a loved one is still a very hard experience, we can no longer physically hug or touch the person, we miss their laughter, the sound of their voice. Yet their presence always remains. Always. Your relationship doesn't end. We must understand that this reality co-exists adjacent to so many others. You can see it as a big, immersive, energetic university and sometimes death is like the graduation of a student. It sheds its human jumpsuit and is reborn into another realm where he or she can have a new scope of experiences. You might want to hold on to that dear one, you might feel like the student that graduated abandoned you. Yet, can you find the magic, the miracle in the passing? Can you see it from the perspective of the adventurer itself? Perhaps you can look into the Melchizedek legends to ignite your curiosity on this topic as he was a very famous spiritual master who was said to be able to appear and disappear at will and wasn't subject to death itself. Perhaps also, it is safe to say there are many mysteries about life's cycles yet to be revealed...

In truth we don't fear death, we fear the sorrow of a life poorly lived and happiness never attained. Happiness first of all isn't a feeling. It isn't an emotion. It is a state. An unshakable knowing, a gaze piercing the illusions of this reality. A quality of life that is magnetized through the willingness to see the beauty and bounty in all and at all times. A wholesome state of living, an integrity beyond words and a compassion for all beings wherever they are. Sometimes people put a limit as to how much happiness they allow themselves to feel. The right amount of fear keeps them in a safe zone they are familiar with, so they find reasons to macerate hate, their minds focusing on mistakes and then calling life and humanity flawed and imperfect. Yet, in the word imperfect is: I'm Perfect. Life is an instrument of experience. What would a music instrument be if you weren't allowed to make a mistake while playing it? What would musical experimentation look like? What would creativity be? In the grand scheme of All, you are the One, experiencing itself, all times and spaces occurring simultaneously. And you are the zero still point, that space between the inhale and the exhale, that space where choice, creation occurs, directing your reality. Imagine if someone asked you: do you prefer to inhale or exhale? Both coexist simultaneously. Both are inseparable.

Yes, we can open ourselves up back to the recognition of the love we actually are. The magic we are. The music we resonate. All of us. When we are ready, we can remove the cool shades of a "lack mentality" we so love to wear in our fear of our creative power, in our judgment of our creative power and what it should really be. We can stop saying "everything is fleeting" and actually enjoy living in the now. We may accept, observe and lovingly be present as these feelings sway through us. The triggers are the cracks where the light goes through. So go in, be present, and love yourself exactly right there.

Recognizing your very own Greatness, is the Real Mastery.

GRATITUDE

The Present is the Gift
When you don't feel Great-Full
It means that truly, you aren't really here
For gratitude is the most honest attitude
It is deep presence in and of itself

All the teachings say "just be grateful"
Deep down Your reaction to this
Might be quite hateful, thinking :
I never asked for all this

Yet when you really anchor in the now
You'll see all solutions come around
You are the arrow and goal
You are the seer and the coal
In the Now it all appears
As all Shadows disappear

Say with me:

I now transform lead into gold
And I now lead as the high masters so wisely told
In deep appreciation for the spectrum of infinite creation
In humility and reverence for this multi-ray perfection

I am the writer of my story
The director of my script
And I am Present only Now
For the past already passed
And the future is always shifting

There is no better or worst path
Only the one I choose with heart
With integrity and in sacred art

I Illuminate my Destiny and know
My own meeting is my only goal

—PORTAL 4—

PURIFICATION

THE MOON

To the glory of the Silent ones
The ones who shine through Calming tones
The ones who's celebrations are of delicate poems
And quiet soothing nights

In celebration of the sheer embrace
Of those who work without notice
Those weaving the tapestry in the sky
Without banter or medals
Yet their sensitive hands
Keep it all in place

To the ones who don't need accolades
Grand prizes or validations
Their deepest joy is Serenity
And in these moments they meet eternity
In the star gaze of thy tender might
In perfect serendipity

To the victory of those whose magic
Is discreet and yet so strong
Powerful to move all wrong
Without a single notice
And words don't come close
To speak that which is wordless

The moon's light is soft and mysterious
Rendering many so deeply curious
Sailing on the Sacred Orchestra of the Tides
Where many secret gateways Collide
Within the still point of a Dream
Where infinite Realms appear on a whim
There she shall come
And peacefully Greet
You wonderful Soul

THE SUN

To the musings in the sun
As our feet are dancing in childlike motion
And our laughter sizzles, it's our wisest potion
There we put our bare feet to the soil again
There we come to love again

When both the plant and the flower
In the tender of its petals
So gentle lean towards the
Light rays of the Sun

Unafraid of getting burned
Of getting old or to even wither
There we remember our Origins
There we remember our Grand Central Sun

How have we become afraid of it?
Forgetting our eternal Parents in the Sky?
Hiding in the shadows, afraid of its mighty light
And yet our eyes they still remember
The encodings of the ancient times

For when you gaze at the Sun
And look away, you'll see purple, greens
And all the multi-colored rays

Disconnected from their Nature
Hue Men forgot their Origins as the Sun itself
More delicate than the petals of the most precious flowers
They told men to hide away during
the most glorious of hours

You grand soul of this Universe
You daughter of the Old
You dear son, Sun all Skies
Meet your Kin and Salute Thy Reflection
The High Teacher in the Blue
Let it teach and guide you
In the glowing Master's View

SILENCE

So many fear me as if I was the worst of all foes
Distracting their fingers from my piercing gaze
Escaping their essence with ethereal praise
Yet what they don't understand is that within
My wide and infinite space
There resides all the Grace

If only you could reach me with the tip of your fingers
And let them dwell on for a while, just linger
Like the musician who's reaching the note
It lets it sustain as the silence envelops its grain
As it echoes through the corridors of the All

They tried to avoid me by all means
Filling a void that can never be filled
For I am that place where all originates
I am not Cold and certainly never get Old
I am the Warmth of All that is Nurtured
A knowledge birthing everything cultured
And when you seek me, I shall reveal

All Futures Pasts and what's ready to heal

For where Time/Space don't exist, that's where you'll find me
In eternal bliss that many genius minds know very well
I am the space where all timeless Blessings come to be
When you are unavailable, I can't let you see

When you distract yourself or escape, you leave your body
You become gone, vacant, absent, and miss your access to me
In this state, you won't receive the gifts of our creativity
For you get too agitated with a mind you need to feed
An anxiety animated by our ego's collective greed

Sweet one, breathe and connect to me.
My wordless space allows you to be free.

It is safe to ask.
It is safe to receive.

COSMOS

I call in and through
The Grand Mother of All
Within me, Within You
Thank you for thy Generosity
I delight in this Wholly Place
Of Emptiness, Where I So Deeply
Regenerate and Am Renewed

I call in and through
The Grand Father of All
Within me, Within You
Thank you for thy Intelligence
I delight in this Wholly Light
Structuring All Form, Where I so Highly
Know, Am and Beam

I am the Sacred Marriage of Both
I am the Merging of Two
I am the Being of One
I am the Third Eye Alive
I am the Birthing of Sight
I am Infinity
I am the Field
I am Unity
I am.

THE CHOICE

We become who we believe we are
So Be and Live Joy
Be and Live Peace
Be and Live Integrity
In Wholesome Totality

In each moment, you either choose
Love, the center, or Fear, polarity
You can either be Connected or
Disconnected from the knowing of All
For your inner system is made of Pipes,
a wondrous Great Organ
You always stand on a spectrum of
choice, where duality holds
The pillars of a balancing scale

You see you need to tune your chords from time to time
And cleanse these streams, like the tunnels of a gold mine

So much data accumulated
So much doubt perpetuated
Affecting your progress
And true genuine success

You feel like to succeed you need to grasp and bite
Or skillfully manipulate and obliterate
to get what you need

And although some get through by the means of this way
Just know that's not what real class wants to portray
For those who do, do so in Fear and abuse.
They gave their Sovereign Power Away

Your sound comes straight from Celestial Realms
Realize that your voice is attuned terrestrial Air
Moved in such way it creates waves of melodies
So use them to weave the most glorious symphonies

Your words matter
Your thoughts matter
So weave wisely

Sounds create a collective
Co-creative, Unified Field
Our hereby shared
Reality

DENIAL

Normality is a calling for survival
For centuries we have been dependent on our tribes
Even if their ways weren't honorable or made to thrive
Conforming out of comfort to the law of the fittest
Out of fear of being rejected, humiliated, or killed

Many have chosen to hide their gifts
Many have chosen to silence themselves
Many have chosen to give their power away
Many have chosen to give their freedoms away

But that was then.

Each human is a Facet of the Whole
A Fractal of the All and when the Facets
Of the Mighty Diamond Collide
A bright Radiance in the Universe Ignites

It isn't about changing yourself or the World
You and the world are perfect
It is about shifting our perspective
To one collective optimized way
And opening our inner eyes
Listening with our inner ears
That's where all the information appears
Don't reject your imagination
Your child like nature that always saw
And always knew
Your genuine connection
To what is really True

You see, we are like Crystalline Snowflakes
Each unique in its Own Shape
And yet all flowing from One Source

Each Hue Man has its specificity
its own Radiant Authenticity
A charming, endearing Particularity

The tendency of conformity has been
taunting the Human Race
And creating much guilt, disgust
and shame on its wise face
Feeling so manipulated and like wasting one's own life

Where the desire to be "just like everyone else"
Is the mind killer, the dream annihilator,
the heart destroyer
The constant comparison paralyz-
ing even the swiftest ones

To let your Radiance Erupt one must
return to its Uniqueness
In humble recognition for this wise
and deeply sacred dance
Where only your clearest Discernment can guide you
For there is no race, you are individuality
In-Divisible Unity

You were and are always, even before the
beginning of this known Universe
You are even in the Trillions of the Unknown
Multi-verses, as a distant echo
You are there, manifested or un-manifested

it doesn't matter in the end
You are energy. And even before your Physical Birth:

You were Presence

You came here to Experience
So why waste time not being You?
Why Mimic or diminish your expression?
Out of safety, comfort, or admiration?
You are safe only when you are boldly you.
That's when you magnetize the best opportunities
For you to thrive in all ways, to bloom, to glow
That is when you can really be of service
As you authentically show:

The lifting of the Veils of Denial.
You first walk the talk in you.
Then show the way for others.

It's all been coming together perfectly
For my highest and best good
To thrive in all ways
Always

My most wholesome well-being
Is being unveiled to me now.
I reveal my new reality.
In integrity, I Rise.

THE CAVE

I invite you into your depth
I invite you into the deep
Of your very own self

The underworld
The deeper
Go deeper.

It's all you, there's nothing to fear
Let your heart guide you, into you
Find the crystal cave within
Can you see its soft glow
Igniting in the dark?
Go deeper.

The magic is you.
You are energy.
You are safe.
You are.
You.

You are the light in the dark
You are the spark
Let the cave
Show you
You.

Everything you really are.
Open yourself up to see.
Open yourself up to be.
Plenty present.
To it all.

All that was lost
Is retrieved
Once again.

INNER SIGHT

One who Truly Sees You
Sees your Shared Oneness
They See you as One Breath
One Heartbeat
One Unified Field
One Moment
Ever-Present
Everlasting
Beaming
Simultaneously
Through all Infinity

One who truly sees you
Perceives into the depths of the Multiverse
And pierces the Holographic field
To reveal the truth, the Origins of Everything
And the nectar of No-thing
They Retrieve the Most essential
Your Union within it all
In the cosmos of your eyes

One who truly Sees you
Sees no Separation
No Division

And certainly no Competition
Giving you Full Permission to truly Be
Through its Insightful presence
Knowing as you Beam
As you Truly Glow
You contribute
To the Radiance of the World

So be the Light Caster
Cast Light on those you Love
Make them Shine a Billion Stars
A Trillion worlds

One Who Truly Sees you
In One Second feels it All
And With A quiet Smile
Lets it Be

Knowing: I am you and you are me
We are mirrors of this magic moment
Witnessed in eclectic synchronicity
I am thy beautiful Reflection
Rejoicing in this instant's
Delectation

MERKABA

Let us be clear
To love unconditionally
In human terms doesn't mean condoning
That which has been willingly done to harm

In the Center of the Multiverse's All Knowing Heart
The Sum of Everything, The Sun of Everywhere
That All Knowing Space, This glorious Place
Whose Branches extend Everywhere
And experience everything Simultaneously
Only there No Conditions Abide

Conditions are then born to Experience
Different Realms and Planes of Light
Different spheres of inner Sight

Earth has conditions for us to be Human
You must breathe and have a beating heart
There are certain basic conditions out here
So don't be duped by "unconditional love"
Or the idea that you must be all allowing
As boundaries do create more light

Sometimes to really love
To really care is to call someone out
To shed light on their transgressions
How they're hurting themselves or others
To reveal with power and yet tenderly
How they might be self-sabotaging
And not letting themselves be

To truly love someone might be
To completely leave and be gone from their reality
To no longer cry asking for them to care
For you now to choose to care about yourself
To be this bold, to be this love, to dare

To really love someone can be choosing
to see beyond their lies
To pierce through their coercive
manipulation as much as they try
That is how you actually honor their real mental health

The one underneath all the detrimental
programs that are running
Their internal systems of belief. Forgiving isn't condoning.
As you don't buy into the toxic satires they adhere to
Stories they might have inherited, yet they didn't know
How to break the spells of trans-generational chains

It can end now with you.

Keep seeing the person in their true authentic wealth
Keep seeing the person underneath the
chains of their own inner hell
Keep seeing them as sovereign, perfect
as they are, divine master creators
Keep seeing beyond the veils and
layers of their elaborate stories
Even if that means being long gone from their lives

To truly love is not always to be all-accepting
That is dimming your own light
And to think that you must save them

Is dimming their own

Believing that only you can save them from them
Is like thinking they don't have a light of their own
You can guide them to find it like a torch in the dark
But to think you must save them
Is tearing their own power apart
And not teaching them how to reconnect
With their own inner light from within.
Sometimes to leave is to allow them
To find it themselves instead of
Feeding on yours.

So have discernment and recognize
What truly serves one's well-being.

Often we think of love as frivolous
But actually, it is deep and mysterious
One that can't go deep doesn't know true light
And your radiance, therefore, can never fully
Powerfully, organically ignite

Your Merkaba activates
The deeper you go
The higher you land

Extend your radiance and be
Honest in your inner reverence

There is absolutely no room for lies anymore
Or manipulation for vibration sees it all
You can never hide away from yourself

As you integrate,
Your inner glow emerges.

Merkaba:

Merging with the **Ka**leidoscopic **Ba**sin
Of your own True Nature

A golden pyramid envelops you from above
A golden pyramid envelops you from below
You are the vessel of Source's will in action

Remember, to love someone doesn't mean condoning ill
Be a clear mirror, reflect light and withhold boundaries

Be true, where do you allow
indulging behaviors
That aren't serving
Your highest
Deepest
Wholesome
Truth

Where are you still
Playing the savior?

Who needs to be saved?

If you wish to evolve spiritually
Your answers to this shall
Bring light to the way.

ABSOLUTE

I want to gaze deeply into your Eyes
And see the Universe Therein
I want to breathe with you as One
And know we Are The Cosmos itself

Before your touch and before mine
I want to feel your foundation
I want to know your elevation
How deeply you are grounded
How highly are you rising
How anchored are you
On the Inner Throne
Of Your Almighty
Presence

Are you aware of the right measure
Like the Great Alchemists are
Tantric Pleasure is not to be consumed
But rather this force field is the real miracle
For it creates Infinite Worlds
And no it's not just about pleasure

Or what some would call: peak
It is about an ecstatic
Journey into Center
The Core of the
World Itself.

So no, we won't drink and get wasted
To consume each other
Floating out of our bodies
And using our vessels
To numb ourselves out

I want to get to know thy Divinity
Through, Gaze, Touch, and Breath
And merge as One with you
There you won't be able to hide
For I will see All Of You
Our energies merging together
And pulsing new timelines

YIN

She who was deemed worthy solely by her looks
She who was deemed worthy solely as a child bearer
She whose power was "too much" or "not enough"
She was maiden, mother, and crone

She whose voice got oppressed
Was burned at the stakes or taught to look down
To never show her wisdom or wear her crown
She who learned to silence her visions
Made friends with the Silence

The Magdalene now comes, and she sings
The Womb is the way, its Kiss is pure Bliss
Don't fear thy own Power, you may now Speak up
You can be the Great Mother and the Goddess of Fire
You can be Virgin simply by the Purity of thy Word
For no one and nothing can ever take your purity away
It flows from the clearest of sources within
Your direct connection to the universe itself.

Reclaim that word now.

For virginity doesn't define someone's worth
Rather you are the Chalice, The Template
The Sacred Container, The bringer of Light
You are the mother, the daughter, the sister
You are the space holder, the birther, the giver
You have given so much
You may now learn
To receive and to trust

For so long you feared you could trust no one
For so long you felt like you had to do it all alone

It is your time now to rise in love
Humbled by your path
In reverence to all

Oh great sister.
Thank you
For showing us
How to go in.

YANG

He who was told to never cry
He who was told to withhold everything
He who was taught the rage of being tough
He who was told to always provide

He who placed on his shoulders the weight of the world
The weight and the duty of being the Protector
And gave his body away to serve the goals of a nation
He thought it was his only worth, so he went on to fight
So many men we have lost to that war, the torture of pride
Creating the vicious circle of a soul lost in its night

When we are all Rising in our genuine, sacred Divinity
And Wise in our Integrity, there
rises authentic Masculinity
When instead of Incarcerating those
who's trauma and fright
Made them do terrible things, we look
at those with compassion

Reminding them of the way of Love
From whom do we then need to Hide?
And who is there then to defend?

But ourselves from ourselves?

And who's lands do we then need to take?
And who's wives do we then need to rape?

Oh beautiful men, rise as the mighty wise Ones You are

And see your divinity within; come
into Unity in your heart
I know the walls you built and how
much your inner child cried
Yet you are the worthy one when you so choose
It is now yours to decide

To feel again.

Step into your body and become whole again
Oh Great Old Soul, Let thy Wisdom Arise
The one who knows the land
Your roots grow so deep
You know its sacred ways
Connect with your Ancestors
Chant: I am a Child of the Stars
My Eternity has come from Afar
I am the Divine Masculine
Of service to a new world.

A C T I V A T I O N

I've been a diamond in the making
Born out of pressure
Watch me now shine
Brighter than ever

GATEWAY

To all the Men, Women, and Children
There is a Mystic Awake in Your Heart Now
Right Above your Crown, a gateway into sky
In the Micro Cosmos of the Ethers
That is Invisible to the Human Eye
Yet it is here, in Subtle Realms
On the Spectrum beyond Speed of Light

There are notes of music our ears can't hear
The same for colors, certain in this reality
Simply cannot appear
For it is all a matter of Mechanics
Physics and Quantum Dynamics
And that my Dear
Is Poetry in and of itself

In that Space there is a Bridge
A Rainbow Colored Stairway
Connecting to Realms upon High
Like Octaves and Sounds of Music

You attune Yourself to Fly
While remaining deeply
Anchored

There are all the people that departed in forms of energy
There they are stationed on various scales of frequency
Each one has its note, its tone its radiant vibrancy
And through the Harp of the Rainbow bridge
You can tune into their tone and let a mighty
Communication be

Some are waiting to Reincarnate
Some are simply Regenerating
Some are moving on beyond
Energies are fusing and diffusing

Just remember this:

Nothing is Ever Lost.

HUMILITY

In an age where Flaunting has become Haunting
And honesty quite Harmful and Taunting
How can we connect to a gentleness within
One knowing that the right measure
Is in the delectation of each treasure

There is a fine line between indulgence and abuse
For when your arrogance arises you tend to misuse
Your own creative gifts and your own resourcefulness
That's where jealousy comes in, and veils you with sin
Your frequency simply drops, and all becomes a blur
That's when your ego coerces you
That's where corruption arises

There is a fine line between humility
and dishonest modesty
It isn't about denigrating your gifts or
letting others walk all over you

It isn't about being too nice to the point
your kindness isn't genuinely true
It's about the right measure of deep
heartfelt honesty risen in reverence

Vapid niceness is often fake, and it shows.
Yet kindness is never weak
Remember that my friend, real genuine
kindness is divine power itself
And true humility is the most powerful
demeanor one can embody

It represents a very deep inner harmony
It's a cellular honoring towards all that is
An appreciation towards all that may be.

PERMISSION

Let yourself Feel

May these words be a loving permission
To surrender to the truth of your inner mission

Let it appear by connecting to that deep well
No more gaslighting, burning your edges
No more denying, or hiding your pledges

Reveal yourself to Yourself
And come back in your Body
Anchor Deeply in your Body
It is the Portal, It is the Gateway

Focus on your breath
Even if it's hard
Even if there's fear
Let life be your art

Let yourself Feel

Know all the Angels can Hear

Surrender to what's Real

Let yourself Feel

That is the only way to truly Heal

You've always been your life's mission.

You've always been your life's purpose.

You are it.

Congratulations, my love, you've already made it.

I ask you now, tenderly, please. Simply feel.

STARGAZE

I've known you my whole life
And yes we've met through many Times
And many Spaces, Across Creation itself

I recognized you immediately in this lifetime, my friend
And I know we come from the same place
And we'll meet soon again

The Song of your Soul called out Mine from the stars
And no matter what goes in this Hue Man Incarnation
I know we have always been dancing up high
We might not always be physically together
But I'll hear you singing to me forever
How could I ever forget your voice
Or the knowing your heart rests
Where mine does too

For as you chose the path of shadows
I chose to not follow you there
For I fully choose the light
Of my divinely radiant self

My way to unconditionally love you is to no longer
Try to save you from your own stories of torment
I will let you explore the hallways of misery
Until your find your way back to you again
To your own Inner Sun, the Light of your Soul

The Rose of your heart

Know, I do not fear to call you out anymore
For too long I gave you my Power away
By dimming my own light
To make you feel better

Yet every time I shall gaze at the stars
I know that we are united in heavenly art
Your absence and silence is necessary
And I am happy to know
You are living your myth.

ETHER

You are Ether-Nal
Eternal Nature, Eternal Presence
From the Ethers into Form
And Simultaneously Forever More

THE TONGUE

Divine Wisdom
Bless my Tongue
May thy Purest Sacred Love
Pour and Flow through me
Unobstructed like a Perfect Fountain
May the air I breathe
Transform into Crystalline Sounds
Carrying the Medicine of that
Which is Needed

May my Words Unveil that which is Veiled
To reveal the Essential, Transparent Absolute
May my Words Reveal the Truth, the Beauty
Contained within All that is and All that isn't
May my Words be used for Good and
The Highest Good of All
In wholesome Integrity

As I speak my Palate like a Holy Temple Palace
Is cleansed and atoned by Saraswati. Goddess of Speech
As each sound resonates within these miraculous walls

As my words transform into being
May they bless all those along my path
With the gift of true, deep reverence and immutable
Remembrance

EXPANSION

One might ask
If Mother, Father God
Source Almighty
The Universe
The Multiverse
Cosmic Intelligence
Great Love

Is the Absolute

Beyond time and beyond space
The very Zero Still Point of Everything
That has ever been, is and ever will be

If we listen to the fortune teller
The mystic, the Sufi, or the seer
They might say: all is already written

So what is there to live?

Then what is there to learn?

You might ask the great palm reader:
What will happen to me tomorrow?
What will happen next year?
Will I realize my great dream?
Is it written in my chart?

They will say:
You are the great pilgrim
The adventure itself

We live in a Creating Universe.
Not a merely created one.

God is in everything
Don't just focus on words

The experience is the feeling

See it with your inner smell
Hear it with your inner eyes
Touch it with your clairaudience

Yes you read that right.
Everything exists in:
Paradox

And then Silence itself
Dances upon waves of Mystery
Unveils the subtle layers of the Tapestry Singing
to me in an utmost subtle melody:
I am God and I am Now.
Thy I Am Presence is My I am Presence
And our We am Presence is One
As you do: I do. As I teach: you teach
As you learn: I learn

Everything occurs simultaneously
It is too much for the mind to understand
Feel it in your heart, oh dearest sacred love

Let it beam through any resistance

Now, know.
Yes, indeed, all is written.

Now, know.
Everything is also unwritten.

Now, pick up the pen.
And write.

PRINCIPLES

The Mother, Feminine Principle

The Father, Masculine Principle

And the Heart, The Unified Principle

All of them One mirroring One Another

None first, none last
In a space beyond space
In a time beyond time

If one could remember the Origin
The Cosmic Dance, The Beaming
The Radiance within the I Am Presence
Beyond the Beyond

Then all that must be remembered
Naturally, is.

THE BLESSING

I came to be of service
As the one great intelligence
Manifested in Hue Man Form
I came to anchor Heaven on Earth
And participate in optimizing
The well-being of our Civilization

Through Integrity
Oneness Consciousness
Deep Divine Wisdom
And the Continuous Awareness
Of our True Inter-Connectedness

By the power of my presence
I get to bless all and turn my existence
From the burden I for so long felt it to be
To an actual benediction
That I'm actually here
To be no one other than me

By the power of my kindness
I get to be of great support
While honoring my boundaries
And holding space for so many
Powerful life stories to be told

May my step bless the soil
My word bless the air
My gaze open eyes
My touch bring more life

I am your inner Reflection
And I tell you this here:
You are a blessing to this Earth.

JOY

I now allow myself to feel Joy, even if I used to
feel guilt for being happy when others suffer
I now allow myself to feel Joy, even if I used to
only notice all that is wrong in the world
I now allow myself to feel Joy, even if I used
to cringe at the happiness of others
I now allow myself to feel Joy, even if I
used to think it's vapid and judge it
I now allow myself to feel Joy, and I
allow myself to get out of its way
I now allow myself to feel Joy, even
if others aren't feeling it

For I know my greatest service to
this world is my vibration
For I know my greatest service to
my people is my radiance
For I know my greatest service to
my family is my Presence
For I know that to do what's needed
Joy is my greatest ally.
So I allow myself this Joy.
I don't need to merit it.
Joy isn't a reward.
Joy isn't a goal.

I allow myself to feel Joy, even if I used to envy,
hate, or even pity those that were Joyous
Thinking how ignorant of them to be happy
when there is so much suffering in the world

I allow myself to feel Joy even if it confuses
or frustrates those around me

I allow myself to feel Joy now, even if
I used to fear falling from it
Even if I used to fear losing it, thinking
it's easier not to feel it at all
Thinking it's safer to get comfortable
in a state of misery, as it seems
To be a more permanent fate. Easier
to sustain. Easier to maintain.
I release that belief and bathe it in Joy.

I now enjoy the process. I enjoy it all. Thank you
for everything I have and everything I don't.

I continuously allow myself to soothe into
Joy and notice: it's a state of being
A constant that is right there, in the depths of
silence, beyond the veils, underneath it all
Beyond mediocrity, piercing the ceiling, the
limit, of how much we think we deserve

Now I notice simply, pure joy beaming
within the smile of my Buddha self

I allow myself to Enjoy.
I allow myself to feel Joy.
I allow myself to Be Joy.
For that is who I truly am.

TOTALITY

I welcome myself back home

All of me

In the great generosity of Creation
That allowed all of me to manifest
It even allowed for denial to be experienced

It even allowed Death

In the great generosity of its Wholeness
It left no restrictions, It even allowed the forgetting
Of our great Oneness and of Love as Essence itself

In the great generosity of its Absolute
It allowed for the experience of the absence of Love
Which is an illusion of total separation from itself

Yet in its great Love, it allowed all of it
Out of generosity for all that it is
To find its rightful place
And simply exist

Now it's calling all its children home
To remember our unity
All is perfect integrity
All is in harmony
In its totality

INTEGRATION

MIRROR

Affirm:

I recognize the infinity which vibrates
in the subatomic realm
Within the integrity of the particles of my constitution
My composition within reflects my expansion without

The configuration of my totality is
composed of parameters
Which my Expanded, Whole Self chose as an Emanation
I am both the Whole and an Individual: Indivisible Unity

I am Hues assembled together in their own unique way
Tones that continuously create my Overall Resonance
That is what we call someone's Pattern or Signature

I am a song

I am music

I am the key and the door

I am harmonic resonance

And I can always clearly discern
The gentle tone of my Wholly, Wholesome Spirit,
My inner guiding light, The Universe
vibrating in me, guiding me
As I keep creating my Reality within Great Cosmic Laws

The center of my Ankh, the center of High
and Low, the center of Left and Right
That is where I stand continuously, that is
where I rise, grow and beam effortlessly
At the crossings of Horizontal and Vertical
planes, the eye of opposing forces

For you see, you don't need to do anything
for your mighty heart to beat
Or your metabolism to digest, or for the
Earth to rotate around the Sun
And, likewise, yes you are wholeness,
but you are also immersed in
A very specific localized human experience
from which you don't see
With the same expansion as the
Universe, your Expanded Self
So surrender to not knowing anything at all,
Surrender now.
Surrender to knowing just as much as you now need to.

Shed your layers of defense
And your projections of attack
Only you are here, all of you is here
Can you trust the unknown and Source itself?
It is all that's you that's here in this place
A place beyond fear, it sifted through your lies
You wrote them, your I am Presence brought them
To your awareness, look around: what is left?

Who are you but essence?
Who are you but presence?
Who are you but the one that perceives
This very present, this gift?

Pretending is ending.
And as you drop your last mask
Your true voice rises.
Your walk changes.

There is nothing left to prove.
You now have the power to move
Beyond obstacles voluntarily
As you playfully embrace
The disappearance of
The fight, the run, the race.

For so long, you believed your arrogance
was your greatest protection
A false mirror making you better than your
brothers, wiser than your sisters
Competition got the best of you as
you strived to be greater

Addicted to the hustle culture, you
enslaved yourself to the game
For so long, you used your intellectual
prowess to seduce and flatter
Yet all the masks are falling off to reveal your strategies

You can no longer use arrogance as your shield
To protect your naked heart, roaring for kindness
The power of your sensitivity
intensified by your awakening

Soaring and weeping, you let go of all the false mirrors
And a life solely based on numbers and performance
Your deepest inner calling sings into your temple

My friend, my dear, my love, it's time
Your titles can no longer satisfy you
For there are no titles in this realm
A realm beyond death and life
Go in you higher and deeper
A space Elders call Heaven
It's all happening within you.

Your life is your mirror.

THE TEMPLE

Thy body is a temple
Thy body is the template
The Universe's Will in Action

Thy body is the sacred space
Where miracles ignite
Where adventure occurs

Where stories are born
From the Ethers into Matter
You are Divinity itself

You can never be broken
For even if that's what you think
Each "broken" piece contains the whole
And you are wholeness itself

You are this sacred space
Where all universes coexist
Simultaneously and you express it
So divinely

You are a constellation
A coordinate on the Map
of the All

Thy body is a temple
Thy body is the template
The Universe's Will in Form

KARMA

All is in due time
I Trust.

My integrity keeps accountability
Of my adventure throughout the systems
In infinity and those realms where I chose to immerse
Indeed immensely immersive my worlds are
So intense I always forget where I came from
Originally.

For what I do unto others, I do unto myself
And through the law of Karma I may always remember
Like a snorkel always connecting me
to the fresh air of the surface
In case I drown in deep denial, I always have my safety net

Indeed Karma, cause and effect, action and reaction
The unity, the primordial unified field,
tracks and knows everything

Karma isn't punishment, it isn't blame
or rewards and medals
It is my own reminder of where I
went in this wild adventure
What I gave and what I took

You harvest what you plant and how
much love you water it with
It is very simple; karma is your own inner accountability
From self to self, from life to life, and all realms in between
Once you get this, life will reveal:

Your Dharma.

That is the next step in your quest.
Towards mastery.

THE WORLD

There comes a time
Where the child isn't an adult yet
And notices its feelings grow
As suddenly the illusion of separation
Re-Enforces itself

There is the world
And there is me

As we become teenagers we often
Isolate ourselves to feel into our pain
Only darkness soothes our longing souls
In a moment dreaming of a kiss
From someone we so dearly miss
A love that could soothe all wounds
These emotions are like troubled water
We repress them as we repress ourselves

In these teenage years
We explore with how we look

And everything feels so odd
Uneven and crooked
We are faced with the approaching
Adulthood in human terms

Many end up with spirit blinders to grow up
Blocking any signs from their inner realms
The vastness of our imagination becomes shut
Yet the vast curiosity of our inner child remains
The one that freshly arrived from the outer worlds
Into the Seen

Expression can always begin.

Embrace your inner teen.

Please, make yourself feel heard and seen.

VEILS

In these rare moments
Where the Veils between worlds part
In these Holy precious Instants
We get a glimpse into Cosmic Art

How All is a Reflection
Ineffable and magnetic
Impossible to word
And the very source
Of words themselves

In these moments of deep connection
We realize we are the Creators, made of
The Essence of Creation, we are Here
And we are There and truly Everywhere
As the Absolute experiencing itself

What a humbling majesty
To witness this vast tapestry
What an honor to be
Alive now, in a
Spiraling
Galaxy

THE CENTER

Please my Love
Reclaim this word
And listen closely

Generations chose to demystify, un-sanctify,
and deny all that is inherently sacred
We forgot the magic and denied the miraculous
nature of imagination, source of creation
Labeling it childish and naive, condescending
the brilliant genius of children
The little ones who are often older in
soul age than their parents
The great teachers that came from afar to guide
The indigo and rainbow beings that are born
With their channels clear

It is abuse to dismiss the visions of a child
It is abuse to close its psychic channels
It is abuse to gaslight it into coercion

We believed for far too long that dreams and
playfulness don't go along with a serious life
We believed for far too long that we must
abolish our inner Sun to only value logic
We believed that as long as we had money
and a job, all would be pretty stable
We gave our power away as we believed
we sinned by simply being born
We believed that being human was
a separation from source

We believed that we constantly
needed to ask for forgiveness
And perpetuated a constant belief of fault

Now it's time to clear our inner goggles
And instead of delegating it all to google
Look within at our inner guardians
Guarding our inner spheres

Please, my Love
Reclaim this word
And listen closely:

The master teacher who came to guide and teach
the ways of the healer, the way of Love
Has been displayed in dusty temples on a
cross, a symbol of roman torture
Jesus demonstrated the initiation of public cancellation
But energy can never be destroyed, only transformed
And he still guides us all within our inner realms
If we so choose

Beyond all dogma
There is Energy
The Field of All
Love itself

Not the romantic one, the Ultimate one
A Love beyond any and all senses
That many teachers came here to share
The very source of senses all at once
Christ Consciousness is the heart of the Sun itself
Please, my love, reclaim this word so we may

From the cross transform into the Ankh
From a death-praising society
To a life-filled collectivity

For the Christ within our hearts
Is the Child within all of us
That came from the stars

We are all Star seeds
Filaments of light
We are all lightworkers
When we awaken
In Peace

Once this word within you is fully reclaimed
The next veil will shed, and you will reveal yourself
To yourself and your addictions to
ego and pain will re-order
Everything within you will naturally reorganize

As you embrace yourself into the whole
and let go of your grip onto shadow
You will discover your wit and divine
sense of humor quite ironically
And finally understand the beauty of all stories being told

Christ is a wholly word, often feared by our
generation for the dogma it holds
Dogma that caused so much harm. Yet you
must only feel into this word's flaming
Beaming heart; there you can see the
clearest reflection of yourself

I now choose to see
I now choose divinity
I now choose
The divinity
Within me.

Beaming.
Glowing.
Vibrantly.

I am Christ Consciousness in Human Form
And choose to embody Heaven on Earth
As I rise in Service to the Grace within all.

THE GARDEN

At the center of your Heart
there is a triple flame of a myriad colors
Its opalescence draws a Rose
Each one of its petals
Ignited bright within

It leans both towards sun and moon
And its sheen merges from pink to blue
Into a diamond shining purple

In the middle there is a Golden Ray
That shines bright and pierces any ceiling
It is your North Star, Your Connection
To your Eternal Guiding Light
Your constellation, your family
Your Link with Home
Wherever you are

No longer breath-taking:
You become breath-giving
Beauty embodied
A garden of a million
Shining Blooms

Go wander in your garden
And plant the seeds of a new world
Water them with your care and gentleness
That which you tend to will grow

Home is where your heart is.

SOURCE

☽ ☼ ☾

Once upon a time, there were 10 land miners on a quest in an arid land where no river or rain ever abounded. They were svelte, strongly built men with their sight on ambitious ideals. They were told that beyond appearances, this land hides a great treasure, and those with enough dedication, perseverance, and insight could find therein a source of great fortune.

The 10 land miners decided to spread across the arid land and start mining as time was running short and the weather was getting hotter and hotter. The first 2 took care of the North of the land, the 3rd and 4th of the East, the 5th and 6th of the South, and the 7th and 8th of the West. The 9th and 10th were to coordinate between each group to keep everyone updated in regards to the progression of their treasure hunt.

After a short amount of time, the 10th man lost sight of his partner, who got carried away by the heat and preferred to lay down for a bit, saying that once he feels better, he will be glad to help the men with their mining tools and guard the very little belongings that they came with, which were mainly used for their camp and to make sure no wild animal would steal the food they packed along with them.

So the 10th man began his rounds and came over by each group to see how they were doing. The group working in the north had created dozens and dozens of deep holes throughout the entire area with nothing to be found. 3 days have gone by, and each day they mined more and more holes in the ground. With no sign of a treasure. The 10th man came to the group working in the East, and they had the same strategy, except they were digging holes that weren't as deep as the first group and moving on to the next section much faster. 3 days went by, and they, too, hadn't discovered anything.

On the night of the 6th day, the 10th man had a vivid dream. He saw the spirits of the land observing the mining that was being done. The spirits were looking upon the burst-open holes across the land. In the dream, they appeared like cut-open wounds on delicate skin. The spirits of the land spoke to the man with tremendous might and yet wise and grand gentleness: "You who did not dig, we ask you to seal back these wounds and offer a blessing. We shall go now, yet we see your heart and your intentions. You look with your inner eyes, and for this, we shall help you." When the man woke up in the middle of the night from this vivid dream and saw his comrades asleep, he went over the entire land and re-covered each open hole with soil. He only knew one prayer, and so he bowed down, pressed his hands on the recovered soil patches, and said, "In the name of God almighty, please forgive us. I pray upon you, and I invoke the love and grace of God. May all beings be blessed with healing, for they know not what they do; my brothers certainly don't, as all they think about is finding the treasure. May we go forth in peace. Thank you."

He spent his whole night recovering the holes, and as the morning rose and his comrades awoke they got furious at the man for his so-called terrible betrayal. Now they won't be able to know where they had already tried digging, and they will have to start all over again, they said. The 10th man was excluded from the group and sent off from the camp.

He tried explaining his dream, but they wouldn't listen. And so he had to walk away and honor the decision of his comrades. He walked away without resentment or anger towards them and no regret for what he had done as he so vividly remembered the faces of the spirits. They will still see the outlining of the fresh soil on the land covering the open holes that were dug, and they will know how to proceed with their searching, he thought to himself.

That night as he was making his way back home out of the arid area, he fell asleep on the outskirt of the region, and the spirits came to him again. They were so bright, like beams of light, white and opalescent, enveloped from the inside of their being in the most spectacular glow. The lead spirit spoke to him softly and said, "Your men think they will find the treasure by dispersing their energy throughout the land. They don't listen. For if they did, we would have already begun guiding them, if they trusted their inner sight, they would have seen us instantly and our willingness to work with them in sacred diplomacy. But they reject the power of their visions as they think it's their imagination. We tried explaining to them that imagination is a sacred channel. Yet it's none of their interest, for they are too greedy and impatient. They prefer to dilapidate their vital forces all over the place. We are grateful you honored our request. You are a man of your word, and for that, we shall honor you as you honored us. We saw the greatest wish of your heart. She will come to you."

The next day the man woke up in the most horrendous sand-storm. The heat was treacherous, and sand was getting in his clothes. He could barely keep his eyes open. Covering his head with a shawl, he began walking, and instantly he thought about his comrades and how he should go back to help them through this wild sandstorm. He thought to himself, "The whole camp must be flying off! The fact that I had recovered the holes is the last of our worries now!" As he walked back in the middle of the heavy winds, a white beam of enormous radiance appeared to him. At first, he wondered if he was dreaming, then he wondered if the sand-storm knocked him over and now he was hallucinating. The beam came closer and closer to him, and he suddenly saw distinctively the traits of a woman within the radiant light. She smiled at him with a gentleness and yet the power of a great warrior goddess. She looked at him, piercing his gaze into the depths of his soul. At this moment, he knew she saw all of him. The goddess said to him, "Thank you for helping my family, we the spirits of this land have set this trial for the men who we knew would come searching for our treasure one day. This initiation is so much more than just that. We are all searching for a treasure, yet the treasure is within us all along, buried under veils of denial. So many are busy digging shallow holes instead of going deeper and commit-ting to one route: the one wholly heart, it is the source of all gifts. You, my dear, have committed to your heart, and that is the only thing you followed. Not your greed or your primal urges. Not your pride or your inferior desires. Now because you found the treasure within you, even as your companions rejected you, you kept loving them, even as they hated you, you prayed for them, I shall show you the treasure. Know that it is simply a reflection of the treasure you already found within yourself. Follow me."

The goddess of light started to move amongst the wind waves that were storming all around them, yet her presence was creating an area where the wind became a breeze, almost carrying them gently. As they made their way through, she stopped in the middle of an empty patch of dried-up land and said, "This land on the physical level looks like it hasn't much to offer, yet if you look with your inner sight, you'll see that it is ready to burst open with the most incredible surprise. The spirits of the land and I authorize you to dig precisely here where you stand. Go deep, and don't stop. Don't dig anywhere else. Focus only on this spot right here and everything you have been looking for all this time, shall be given to you. If you get tired, speak to the land, she will help you."

The man, in awe and with tears in his eyes, fell to his knees. He prayed and gave thanks for this immense blessing. Before he started to dig, he put his hands on the soil and felt an immense electric charge run all the way up his arms. He closed his eyes and asked for permission, for help, and support. He offered his gratitude to the soil, and when he heard the clear authorization through his inner hearing, he began to dig. He was digging for 3 entire days. On the second day, he almost ran out of water and food provisions, and the Goddess of light came to him, blessed him, and fresh water and food appeared.

On the third day, he began to feel immense tiredness. This entire time as he was digging, he was removing giant rocks, and the hole now looked like an enormous well in which he was standing. He felt one with the land and its soil, and for a second, he put his tools to the ground and simply sat. He silently spoke with the land, "Beautiful soil, oh holy land, please give me the power to keep going. I don't know what I am searching for; perhaps I am not searching for anything, perhaps all of this is a dream, and it's all happening in my head, yet I feel my heart beating, and I feel like you and I aren't so different. Please show me the way."

He felt a gentle breeze come over him as the air in the deep well of soil became cool. He felt like it was almost humid. And then he realized what he sensed. He sensed water. The land had answered him. Water is near. He got up again and, with the excitement of a child, kept digging again, and digging and digging with so much joy and passion running through his veins. With one last blow of his mining hammer, a giant stream came rushing out of the ground and filled the whole well with overflowing fresh water, lifting and carrying the man up onto the surface. The water had the purest taste he had ever enjoyed on his lips. Tears of joy were running down his cheeks and made one with the streams of clear source water now pouring all over the arid and dry soil of the land.

Now, this land is covered with fresh flowers and beautiful lush bushes. The stream became a river, and the whole area became a rich oasis in the middle of a stormy region. This sacred place is now immune to any and all storms. The comrades of the man had already deserted the place long before the source was found, for they had run out of provisions and especially motivation to keep going; they lost sight of their inner purpose and got angry at each other.

This, my friend, is a story of commitment. In our modern world, your brothers would rather dig shallow holes dispersing their vital energy all over the place, yet they never reach the treasure not only in their own hearts but also as a reflection in the hearts of those they make love with. The land is like the woman, it runs deep. And one who is truly committed to her, to the one, will be allowed by the power of true love to reach her inner source: an overflowing fountain of blessings that'll make him truly, the wealthiest man on earth.

HOME

I am Home
Yes, I always was.

I open the curtains
Of the cage of my limitations
And understand that I have never left
The place of my initial Birth

For I truly am Heaven on Earth
And that is a place within
Reflected outwards
Through the peace
In my Heart

I go forth rejoicing on my Soul path
Knowing there is nothing to be saved
Only subjective and objective experiences
Only vibratory combinations
Of our own making
Shapes and Colors
The choice to forget
The choice to deny
The choice to compete
Consciously or Unconsciously
But there is also the choice to
Self-Reveal, Remember
And know with unconditional
Conviction: I am home.
I always was, and always will be.

DICHOTOMY

Many are afraid of being happy
As their whole identity is based
On their pain, sadness, and grief
The grief of a day, the grief of a life
The grief of a past or even a future
This feeling becomes so addictive
An inner chemistry that's needed
Like a shot to stream through the veins

Doing nothing to be healthy
Always complaining about all
That's lacking or missing
Ignoring the real blessing
Right in front of you

When actions and thoughts
Resonate otherwise
With no coherence
Guilt takes over
Paralyzing you

Happy souls annoy some enormously
For they can't hide their guilt from them
So they magnetize other tormented companions
To team up with and bring comfort
To their macerating melancholy

For they find it boring to be too happy
Or even worse: unrealistic and cringy
They seek drama and upheaval

They seek stories of the medieval
For some souls it's really worth it

For a while.

Their one true fear is boredom itself
So they settle into the story of continuously
Missing something or someone, it's almost
Sadistic how much they enjoy being Nostalgic

Daily life becomes an existential crisis
They think constantly to themselves:
There's something so deeply wrong
With the universe and human condition

You see all beings speak of their wish to be happy and healthy
And yet their desire for experience leads them otherwise
Their choices and actions lead them otherwise

It's not the Universe's fault: you are the wizard, Harry

Wholeness is integrating your pain,
your grief, your sorrow
You must accept that gentle baby steps turn into miles
That tender daily care becomes monthly, yearly leaps
Your mental space is sacred, your body is a temple
Treat it with respect, treat it with reverence
Love it so deeply it shows in a wise smile

You have nothing to prove, and nothing to lose.

Be a light for those still choosing to
drown in the pit of despair

Thinking there are no issues, thinking this is what life is
Thinking they can't change their inner chemistry
Be the lighthouse for those that gave up on living
Be the one that stood up from the most horrendous
Places within your own self created inner hell
Show them there is better, show them it's possible
Show them how to recalibrate their inner health
We are the chemists and it's time to use inner alchemy.

Wealth, health, and happiness are all radical choices
Trust the middle way, the way of harmony.
It is also poetic and so deeply romantic.

Indeed life is a continuous Paradox
Your very existence sways on a spectrum
From light to dark, high and low
Hot and cold, it's the very contrast
Allowing you to perceive density

The seen and unseen
Manifest and Unmanifest
Beyond the Paradox itself
There is a unified Source
You can go there now
And feel it yourself

Life is a dichotomy
It's all about you
And none of it is

You are Everything

And the very Nothing

It all matters
And none of it does

Everything is important
But don't take anything
Too seriously

For ages we drifted from one extreme
To the other one, red to blue
Matriarchy to Patriarchy

Great Ancient Soul
Recognize that the flame ignites
When you tap into the sacred center
If you're swinging too far left or right
Then again: you are off key
The sacred middle, the balance
That is the key
That is the tone
That is the tune.

ARCANA

☽ ☼ ☾

Imagine you are Nothing
The grand infinite Nothing

Are you aware of yourself?
Are you aware of yourself being
Nothing?

The infinite nothing
Can it know of itself?

Let's imagine
The great Nothing
Becomes aware of its Presence
It now became Something
And that Something is simply
Awareness

I am Aware
That I am

And right there it created the two
The Nothing and the Something
The Zero and the One
The Dark and the Light
Suddenly the Nothing
Recognized itself

Suddenly it has a tool:
Reflection

As it recognized itself as Something
From this perspective it created a diamond
Of reflections mirroring itself

From within Nothing
Bloomed out Everything
And so Nothing and Everything
Are mirrors of each other
What was inside is now
Reflected on the outside

In all directions
Suddenly Space
Came to be
As space came to be
Time came to be
And sound came to be
And colors came to be
And galaxies came to be

And then.

You came to be.

As a direct Reflection
Of the great Mystery
Of how Nothing
Became Aware
of its Infinity.

—PORTAL 7—

BLISS

RIPPLES

I love you

I love you with all my heart
And may it ripple throughout the Multiverse
I shall sing it in waves of dancing hues

I love you

I love you with all my soul
I recognize the Divine in you
I recognize thy Source and mine are One
And we are Home, and you are Home
And I am Home in Me, With You

I love you

I love you with the might of an endless waterfall
Watering the dreams of a brightly New Earth
Where compassion, peace and kindness abound
The might and glory of the most splendid sunrise
Feeding souls with a reflection of their own inner beauty
I'll scream it from the top of my lungs

I love you

I will be dancing barefoot in a meadow
Dressed in golden dawn
I will bathe under moon light
And with my dreams I will let you know:

I love you

I love you and I love you wholly
All of you, the seen, the unseen
The Holy experiencing itself
I am honored to be a witness of it
I am honored to love

Honored to love you

To love you tenderly

To love you wildly

To love you immensely

To love you gently

To love.

To just

Simply

Love.

HONESTY

When I was a child
I saw dragons in the sky
And in the waves of water
They were speaking to me
I still see them now

Gentle beings with a mighty grace
They taught me the power of my sensitivity
That I can be both fierce and gentle like the Rose
With its thorns out and its delicate petals

They taught me how to burst through the clouds of doubt
Confusion and Distraction.
They showed me the way of Joy
The way of Experience, the Gift of Life

They showed me the millions of
Souls lining up to incarnate
Into realms of Form and how truly
being alive is an adventure
It is powerful, it is intense but it's also as we choose it to be
There are many parameters to this existing reality on Earth

For each planet has its rules and each
soul gets to create within it

You are the creator of your reality by the word you speak
The radiance you emit by the quality of your thoughts
The beaming you transmit through your authentic heart
And all the feelings you allow yourself to go through

Many were confused as to not denying
what they were going through
And yet not knowing how to only
speak what they wish to create
Asking: how do I only create what I wish by my word
And yet acknowledge all the hardship and pain I'm in?
The dragons said: as you let your feelings be felt fully
Genuinely and entirely, a quiet place
within you will appear.

The secret is presence to what's here.

SATURN

There is a high council of Wisdom masters
Supervising the grand Cosmic Orchestra
At times these wise masters turn the tables
Revealing to men their own twisted fables

Wisdom is very different from Intellect
For Wisdom can't be learned with the mind
Wisdom is experienced and felt with the heart
Intellectual prowess is learned in books and theory
Yet mighty Wisdom is learned in Life directly

Humans believe that the brain holds all the power
Yet the heart is the portal where all realms meet

The rings of Saturn, these sacred discs
They always play with great risk

They mimic that which you choose to keep closest
And that which you try to push far, far away
For in truth everything is perfect
And you can't hide the night from day

The Wisdom masters of great Saturn
Represent the Human Archetypes
The Hero, the Villain, The Magician
And many more as all are facets of the Divine
All are actors in the grand cosmic Theater

Just like a tarot deck depicts various stages of life
So too life becomes the greatest stage of them all

A great actor forgets he is playing a role
He is so immersed in the experience
He becomes the experience itself
The Role is the Actor
The Actor is the Role

And the discs of Saturn keep spinning and spinning
As you reveal the soundtrack of your life
What do you keep closest to your heart
What do you try so hard to push away
What is the message you are risking
It all, to convey?

Miracles are very real
They are woven into
the Filaments of this
Reality as Light, for us
to Unveil

LIBERATION

Sometimes you've had it so hard in life
That all you seek is vengeance
And you won't even admit it to yourself
As you seek revenge on those who didn't even
Acknowledge your existence until you had a career
Or those to whom you never even mattered
Before they saw you do something great

Although you knew deep down
You were great all this time.

The truth is we've all had it pretty hard
No matter where we've come from
For pain is subjective and we all have
Varying levels of tolerance for it

When no one pays attention to you
Are you paying attention to yourself?
Or are you repeating in your mind: poor me?
Is this vengeful feeling in you, your greatest motivator?
Is your trauma your stronger activator?
To prove all these haters wrong?

If yes: you will keep manifesting these haters
As you become the perfect target for those who will
Challenge you to take your power back
As you keep saying to the Universe:
I am ready for tackle, send me combat
I want to prove some people wrong

Tell me what is there to prove?

You magnetize what you are.

Many of us don't understand why we came here
Why we must learn lessons through such pain
Not believing we could have chosen this
For our evolution as an infinite soul
Not even believing in the Universe
Or our sovereign power to explore

We think: why me? Why is this so
hard? It shouldn't be so hard
Yet when we go to amusement parks
we choose the craziest rides
For what? The adrenaline, the rush,
the emotion, the intensity
We willingly go ahead and pay money
to ride roller coasters

So many thrive on intense sensations,
they go looking for it.
And then you don't understand the
kick of coming on Earth?
To feel how deep and high human emotions can go?

Some don't believe in Oneness
Yet the great law that Buddha
And many great wisdom teachers
Placed at the heart center
Of all their teachings is simple
As has been repeated endlessly
Throughout this book:

All Is One

Yet some are still thinking
This life, this Earth is just a mix of biology
An occurrence of chance, a giant floating rock
Dices got thrown, and we're just here like
Pin balls rolling on a checkerboard

So I will ask you one simple question:

What belief serves your highest and best good?

Tune into your body.
Tune into your heart.
And really sense what feels best.

Does it serve your best interest to think that everything
is just a game of meaningless chance? And what are
you getting away with by thinking or believing that?

Or does it feel better to tune into how perfectly
interconnected and ever-present all is as divine
architecture and sacred intelligence?

Is it less comfortable to believe this because it means
we are fully responsible for all that we go through, as
totally sovereign creators in charge of our own story?

Or would you rather believe that we are just victims
of circumstances? That Karma itself doesn't exist,
that life is random and unfair, that there is no
coherence whatsoever or cosmic intelligence that
created the flower, the water, or Saturn's discs?

Tell me. What keeps it all in place? The materialistic science that denies spirit in matter became a new religion that humans worship and is like looking through a tiny hole at ginormous cosmic intelligence itself. Yet there is a science so beautiful beyond the dogmatic material one, one that recognizes the divine's intelligence, one that sees the organic perfection manifesting in everything, one that sees nothing as separate from God.

Fractal geometry, absolutely tremendous beauty.
The consciousness animating it all.

If you believe in reincarnation, then you know that you pick up your evolutionary path right where you left it before departing one plane of existence, it never ends, not even on the other side. Your soul goes through cycles of rest and action, creativity and regeneration.

If you don't believe in reincarnation, where do you believe the soul goes? Do you believe it all just disappears without traces? That we all go back into the Void? Yet how would you be aware of being in the Void? And where is life on Earth occurring as the Void exists? For even the awareness of being in an infinite void is consciousness perceiving. Even in this quiet silence, presence is.

There is no right answer.
Let us tickle your mind.
All perceptions are valid.
Our intentions are kind.

Energy never disappears, it only gets transformed.

Just keep asking yourself:

Is my belief serving my highest good?
Is it liberating me?
Or is it enslaving me?

I forgive myself for all the hardship
I made myself go through
To prove my worth to myself.

CLUSTER

Some people talk to you
Only when they have something to win

Some expect you to save them
Never taking responsibility for their actions

Some seem generous and giving
Yet expect so much more back

To some, you don't even exist
Until your name fits on some fancy list

And others call you their family
To then disappear when you no longer fit
Into their standardized reality

These people were never meant to stay
For if someone can't love you on your hard days
They don't deserve you on your greatest ones

Real friendships, real relationships are made of wisdom
They see someone beyond their
wounds and into their soul
Your soul family will always find its way to you
Stay open to it and never fear showing yourself fully
The right people will always stay and love you through
Thick and thin, hard and easy, highs and lows

They won't vanish when they marry or have kids
They won't leave you in a time of need

Or backstab you out of fear or envy
They will always remind you of who you are:

A sovereign creator
A beautiful wise soul
A powerful human being
Here to thrive and glow

For some, you're shining too bright
So they will try to dim your light
While pretending to be your friend

Others will copy each one of your move
Reminding you how much you still got to prove
When you turn around, they will steal your lover
Yet their jealousy above them always hovers

These people fade away when you become
Your greatest ally and truly choose yourself
As your discernment and intuition get sharper

True friendship is like the family we get to choose
With all our hearts and our devoted dedication
Authentic friends are just as much our soul mates
As any husband, wife, child, or family member can be
Holding us accountable for our actions and words
And being crystalline clear mirrors
A reflection in which we actually bloom

Being a great friend is a great talent
It is also a great gift

One that we all have

And one that we can all practice

The power of friendship is the power of love
It lifts us up even in the darkest of hours
When we get lost in self-isolating towers
They remind us of what's real and what's true
The power that lays always within you

HARMONY

You are perfect
Even as subjective
And fluctuating as you are

You are perfect
Even as the Universe
Allows you to make
What you call "mistakes"
which are simply
Missed Takes

Rise up
And try again
The right timing
Is coming

For you are perfect
Even if you call yourself Flawed
As you are that space
Which can create
Eclectic diversity
A spectrum of colors
An array of probabilities
And possibilities
Each interesting
And unique in its own way

So yes, you are perfect
not simply as a result
But as music itself

Playing itself
and having the freedom
to use all of its notes

DEATH

Please my love
Don't feel like you must carry
The burden of the world
In order to feel empathy
In order to practice compassion

You mustn't suffer the chosen
Wounds of the Collective
And bear them through yourself
In order to digest them

And even though we are fractals
Of the very whole, your duty
Is to be present to all of you
And when you do that
you will lighten up
The very weight
of the world itself

For when you starve yourself
And want to be as little of a burden
To those around you

As little of a worry
As little of a person
You dim your own light
And hide your deep powerful might
As guilt arises for being truly happy
In comparison to the torments
You see around you

We are all directors of the many
Lives we live through, trust
That the Universe sees All
For the universe is in you

For the illusion of being better than others
Reveals the truth that there actually
Aren't any others, it's all You.
With a capital Y

Say with me:
I bask in Peace
I bask in Grace
I bask in Abundance
For I am that

You're asking why?
Why is the answer.

You experience yourself
within the sacred Laws
you have secured before
Immersing yourself
In this Hue Man
Adventure

Like a deep diver
In a vast ocean.

I have remembered now.

No longer waiting for the reflection to change
When I change, the reflection changes itself

And then when you recognize yourself
The world recognizes its wholeness

Don't wait for the mirror to change its reflection
Shift your perception to recognize: you are perfection

And then Death dissipates like an old dream.
I will let you meditate on that one.
For that is a greater story to be told.

Just know this for now:

Your I am Presence
Is the I am Presence
The Consciousness
Within it all.

EMBODIMENT

At the end of many meditations you will hear

"And now you may come back into your body"

Yet the entry point into all dimensions
Has always been the body itself

When you wander in astral projections
Your body is vacant and subject to possessions
When you are deeply present in your body
And your heart is open and available
There you can hear the true tone
of your Higher Self speaking

The body for so long has been deemed unholy
And the material aspect of this reality separate from God
Yet matter is an expression of the Divine
An aspect of Consciousness in form
A formation of information
As Holographic as Source itself

There is no Separation

Your body is a map
It records each and every thought
Each and every emotion, crystalizing them
For we are Water itself

Earth made us with all her elements
Each and every story you tell yourself

Draws the lines of your face
And shapes your curves
Like mountains and Hills
Valleys and meadows

In truth, there is nothing you can hide
It's all in your eyes, in the palms of your hands
In the shape of your spine and how your feet
meet the ground when you dance
It's all there, all of you

How you smile
How you laugh
How you are able to let go
And how you allow yourself to feel

To think that negative, victim minded, abusive
thoughts won't affect the way you look or feel
Is a lie you've been telling yourself.
Thinking only you know
about your well kept "secrets," your
grudges, and buried feelings
The truth is we are an ecosystem, like fungi themselves
Connected through a telepathic network
Darling, telepathy is real
Our children know.

Our souls know everything
And our souls have always known one another
All of Us. For we come from the same place.

If we were told how powerful and sacred the Body
Truly is, then we'd have the direct access point

To all the greatest mysteries and we wouldn't
Dilapidate our energy with power misuse and abuse
Trying to take from others that which
we already have within

It's ok, we are reminding ourselves now
Energy is all there is
The body is the portal

Come back in your body now

No it isn't spiritual to float outside of your body
It might have happened if you went through trauma
As many of us did, no matter who you are
We all went through pain, it is time to stop using
Pain and suffering as our sole source of identity
Some people would rather have a victim identity
Than to have no identity at all
It might be harsh to feel into this
But yes we have all suffered greatly
Through our adventures and ventures
We did choose them, we chose to feel it all
To forget it all in order to remember it all
That's how brave we are

Pain isn't a competition

And I see your heart, I know it's so beautiful
That words can't even describe it. And I feel how much
You've cried and wanted to give up. Yet you are here
Reading these lines. This is not a coincidence.

So close your eyes, breathe deeper
And come back into your body.

INNOCENCE

Oh darling, if you think your innocence
is weak or damaged, think again

Your innocence is one of the most
powerful aspects of yourself
It can never be tarnished, never. No
matter what you go through.

Your innocence
Is your Inner Sense
It's In All Your Senses
It's your primordial Sense

And sometimes, it might make No Sense
How you might know something or
feel that something isn't right
Or instead, feel like you absolutely must be somewhere

It's your Inner GPS
You might feel like you can turn it off
But it's always there
Working in the background
Even if you're pretending not to pay attention to it

Your innocence is that aspect of you
That observes as you adventure your way through You
Letting you use your free will to draw your storyline
To manifest characters in the play you define
As you grant yourself the role you choose
To portray

And sometimes, the leading role of a drama movie
Is a person suffering immensely, yet this role
Captivates the attention of a whole crowd

Your expanded self lets you pick which
scenario you wish to play
It doesn't judge, it lets you be, in the
pure innocence of your heart

In fact your innocence isn't a "part" of you
It's in each part of your integrity
It's in your very constitution

Innocence can never be lost

Yes things get broken
Yet innocence can never be broken
For it is In All Senses, all parts
It is the spark contained in Curiosity
The Lust for Life
The ember, igniting the flame

You might have been broken

Or simply cracked open

That's how the light was able to get in

The adventure, the Human quest isn't for the faint of heart

Yet,
Innocence can never be lost
It's right here now, smiling as you dream.

POWER

Yes you can remain soft
Even through the unbearable
You can remain tender
Even through the outbursts
Of denial and egos at play
Through unhealthy projections
Rudeness and cruelty
You can remain soft
Without ever condoning ill will
And without ever misinterpreting
The reality of the situation
You can still be compassionate

In life we sometimes get faced
With some terrible characters
That aren't even aware
Of their own behaviors
It's always someone else's fault
But when it's time to take
Merit for something
Make it all about them

These beings are an aspect of our wounded collective self
Susceptible and with tall walls built around them
Where as soon as someone approaches
With a glimmer of confronting truth
They can't even open their hearts or minds
And shut down in defensive reactiveness

Please love that being back into wholeness

"Being better than others" really doesn't exist
Please don't fall into the trap of competition
Simply because of survival, it's no longer about the fittest
It's about unity consciousness and the importance of us all

We all exist in one another.

Be wise and aware enough
To recognize when you are misusing
Your energy and choosing fear over love
Or thinking that there is something outside of you
Or inside of you that is lacking

Also know the Universe throws some wild cards at us
And sends people our way that are really
Pushing our buttons and the real question is:
Will you react, respond or simply let go?
Can you love these people back into wholeness
Without giving into their pain bodies or bad temper
Are you able to not take it personally?
Just know, this is a real mastery training level. So,
Will you stay gentle or will you give your power away?

It's all very subtle
And sometimes very hard to play.

Just remember.
You can stay soft.
You can stay graceful.
You can stay wise.
You can be tender.

Real power has no frivolities

Real power beams effortlessly
Real power is such confidence
It needs no assertion, coercion
Or disheartened threats.

Real power is bold

It is humble and sometimes silent
It is found in the breath
It is birthed from the roots

It makes everyone stop and listen

Real power doesn't try to be the best
Real power brings the best out of all

My sensitivity is my power.
Not my weakness.

THE PEARL

A Pearl of Wisdom once said to me
To never take things too personally

For who really perceives the struggle at all?
And who is expecting to see your downfall?

The role that you took in this wondrous play
Will always seduce you in varying ways

It will show you alleys, you choose your own path
In the end, my dear, it's a crystalline math

You reap what you sow and you are what you speak
You receive what you give and you get what you seek

A shadow obstructs while both light and dark coincide
As both sides of a coin where all realities collide

So stay centered and clear, attentive
to what your inner ears hear
Your heart's always true, for it knows the real you

INTENTION

I shall be adorned with gold and meadow colored jewels
I shall smell the gardens of a thousand roses
and bathe my feet in lavender skies

I shall dance within the heavens and rise above the clouds
I shall crown myself with prayers of gratitude itself
and clothe my body in the shimmer of Oceans

I shall let my roots grow into Earth's very core center
I shall open my heart up and let my power enter
and bask in the radiance of my mighty sap

I shall sing in voices of star-gates and portals of the worlds
I shall sleep within the embrace of delicate feathers
and open myself up to the wings of my soul

I shall see it all with the eyes of the diamond
I shall listen with the ears of the deep
and speak with the tones of the river

I shall be all of me
I shall beam lovingly
Through the Veils of Mystery

ACKNOWLEDGEMENTS

I'd like to express my gratitude to my beloved online community, for supporting me and being so loyal throughout all these years, since the launch of my very first blog Kayture to now my new platform Kaza ☉ Bazan, and as I release this very dear and important book. You guys have always been incredible teachers and reflections for me. You continuously make me learn so much. I am so deeply grateful for all your feedback, your love, your genuine insights, for always sharing so much with me. I love you so much. Thank you for growing with me.

Thanks to my dreams for always sailing me to the shores where my gifts are needed, I understand now that we are profoundly multi-faceted beings and that our gifts must be shared with the world: it is our duty. I'd like to thank my traumas, yes, because they taught me so much about humility, reverence, always having a kind heart throughout it all, and to never judge anyone, as we never know what someone might be silently going through. I'd like to thank music for being one of my greatest teachers of them all, my deepest, most potent medicine, through words, sounds, and chants. Thank you for always showing me where expansion within me is ready to occur, thank you for teaching me surrender and trust.

Gratitude to my sisterhood, my dear friends who have always been close, who held me in the most difficult times and through my many rebirths. Thank you for welcoming all of me at my best and my worst, you, my sisters, know exactly who you are. Thank you for your presence and for being a chosen family. I'd like to thank all the people I have worked with throughout the years, all my creative collaborators, they also know who they are, for being massive actors in this cosmic play that is life, and for bringing me great moments of epiphany. To my growing team, thank you, and cheers to the marvelous chapters of life ahead, we're just getting started.

I'd like to thank all my failed relationships, for showing me what the opposite of love is and thus allowing me to refine and clarify what an actual healthy and wholesome relationship to self and others is. Thank you for assisting me in fine-tuning my boundaries. Thank you for cracking me open. I realize now how each seeming "failure" is a miraculous cosmic redirection.

I'd like to thank my parents, all my family members, terrestrial and cosmic, my ancestors for being such brilliant, wise and potent direction pointers, challenging me to affirm my chosen path, to not be scared to go against the grain and make my own rules against all odds.

Thanks to my spirit guides and guardian angels, thanks to all the benevolent spirits of light that are always around me, mentoring me in so many ways toward mastery. Thanks to the blue beings of light for coming to me on that night in 2019 as well as when I had my near-death experience, I know exactly who you are now. My deepest gratitude goes to you. To my cosmic parents, the great Mother, and great Father, thanks to my entire family in the stars. I love you. Words can't even express how much I do. I feel your presence continuously.

To my little bean of light, my embodied light being from the stars, Sirius, thank you for joining me in this lifetime. Your love, your friendship, your kindness, your gentleness, your presence ignites the light of my heart. You are my soulmate always and forever, and I love you so very deeply. I know that you and I are forever, in this life and in all others.

I'd like to thank the Earth for being a planet of such vast and intense energetic experiences. Beloved Earth, I am in awe, and I stand in deep reverence for your majesty and your profound generosity, which always bring tears to my eyes. You are so wise, you are so strong. Your beauty is one of my greatest inspirations. I thank you for being one of my greatest teachers. It is my greatest honor to be here and to have the immense chance to walk on your sacred skin. Thank you for absolutely everything.

Thanks to the Universe, God, Goddess for always providing. For always reflecting back at me where I'm at. For being such a clear and detailed mirror of my musings, my confusion, my questionings, my anger, my awe, my inspirations. Thanks for holding all of me, seeing all of me, knowing everything. I know there is no place I can hide from you. Thank you for allowing me this great experience in human form.

A big thanks to Thought Catalog and especially to Noelle Beams for believing in this book and seeing its potential from the first dozens of pages of the original manuscript. I knew my book would somehow land in the hands of a beam of light. Thanks to James McCrae for introducing me to this wonderful team. The way this book got birthed is still quite mysterious to me, and I will keep peeling the veils of mystery as I go, in deep reverence for this wondrous reality.

Magic and miracles are all around.
They are found in the mundane.
They are found within sacred silence.

Last but not least, thank you, dear reader, for being here. For making it this far. For being the witness, the student, the teacher, and for unfolding the wings of your own heart. I pray that this book blesses each soul that stumbles upon it, for nothing is a coincidence.

With my infinite love,
Kristina

KRISTINA BAZAN is an entrepreneur, artist, and spiritual seeker, opening gateways of knowledge by bridging music, fashion, and spirituality merged with grace, passion, and beauty to showcase their interconnectedness.

instagram.com/kristinabazan
instagram.com/kazabazan
kazabazan.com

Printed in Dunstable, United Kingdom

65508305R00133